# Body Language

## A Ultimate Psychology Guide to Analyzing

*(The Secret Science of Speed Reading People to Influence Decisions)*

**Edward harris**

Published By **Oliver Leish**

## Edward harris

All Rights Reserved

*Body Language: A Ultimate Psychology Guide to Analyzing (The Secret Science of Speed Reading People to Influence Decisions)*

## ISBN 978-0-9948326-9-6

No part of this guidebook shall be reproduced in any form without permission in writing from the publisher except in the case of brief quotations embodied in critical articles or reviews.

Legal & Disclaimer

The information contained in this book is not designed to replace or take the place of any form of medicine or professional medical advice. The information in this book has been provided for educational & entertainment purposes only.

The information contained in this book has been compiled from sources deemed reliable, and it is accurate to the best of the Author's knowledge; however, the Author cannot guarantee its accuracy and validity and cannot be held liable for any errors or omissions. Changes are periodically made to this book. You must consult your doctor or get professional medical advice before using any of the suggested remedies, techniques, or information in this book.

Upon using the information contained in this book, you agree to hold harmless the Author from and against any damages, costs, and expenses, including any legal fees potentially resulting from the application of any of the information provided by this guide. This disclaimer applies to any damages or injury caused by the use and application, whether directly or indirectly, of any advice or information presented, whether for breach of contract, tort, negligence, personal injury, criminal intent, or under any other cause of action.

You agree to accept all risks of using the information presented inside this book. You need to consult a professional medical practitioner in order to ensure you are both able and healthy enough to participate in this program.

Table Of Contents

Chapter 1: Micro-Expressions And Subtle Signals ......................................................... 1

Chapter 2: Navigating Personal Space In Business Settings ................................... 15

Chapter 3: Reading And Using Vocal Cues ............................................................................. 22

Chapter 4: Building Rapport And Trust ... 29

Chapter 5: Take A Calm And Confident Posture ................................................. 43

Chapter 6: Show Genuine Warmth ........ 60

Chapter 7: Adapting Body Language For Remote And Virtual Communication ..... 74

Chapter 8: Convey Interest And Honesty 92

Chapter 9: Maintain Moderate Eye Contact During Conversation ............................ 103

Chapter 10: The Power Of Nonverbal Communication ................................... 115

Chapter 11: How To Interpret Facial Expressions And Gestures .................... 123

Chapter 12: Mastering Your Own Body Language ............................................. 135

Chapter 13: Body Language For Negotiation And Sales........................... 145

Chapter 14: Conquering Public Speaking ........................................................... 153

Chapter 15: Navigating Different Cultures ........................................................... 163

Chapter 16: The Dark Side Of Body Language ............................................. 167

Chapter 17: The Foundations Of Nonverbal Communication ..................................... 175

Chapter 18: Understanding The Role Of The Eye-To-Eye ..................................... 178

Chapter 19: Strong Correspondence .... 181

# Chapter 1: Micro-Expressions And Subtle Signals

Micro-expressions are short, uncontrollable facial expressions which occur as a response to emotion thoughts or events. They typically last for under a half-second and may reveal a person's real feelings even if they attempt to cover their emotions. The ability to recognize and interpret micro-expressions could give valuable insight into the emotions and thoughts of other people, especially when verbal messages aren't clear or consistent.

Finding Micro-Expressions are infrequent, you have to be extremely attentive and focused in order to recognize the micro-expressions. Be attentive to the facial expressions, particularly those around the mouth, eyes and eyebrows. Take a look at people's faces during different situations, like watching a video or having conversations to improve your skills to detect small facial expressions.

Interpreting Micro-Expressions:

When you're in a position to recognize micro-expressions it's important to read the meanings accurately. Be aware that micro-expressions may be incorrectly interpreted. Therefore, you should consider the context as well as other non-verbal clues prior to drawing conclusions. Learn the seven universal facial expressions as well as the emotions associated with them to aid to interpret the micro-expressions accurately.

Subtle Signals:

Alongside micro-expressions, individuals can also exhibit subtle signals to show the emotions they are experiencing or their thoughts. They could be subtle shifts in the color of their face and pupil dilation as well as sweating. Being aware of these subtle signs can give more information about how an individual's emotions are affecting them or reaction to specific situations.

Context and Consistency:

If you are interpreting micro-expressions or subtle signals, it's important to take into account the context of your observations and be sure your interpretations match with the rest of your verbal and nonverbal clues. If the micro-expression is not in line with what the person is saying this could suggest deceit or that the individual does not like the subject that is being debated. Make sure to be cautious when you interpret and don't jump into conclusions without taking a look at the entire situation.

## 3.3. The Role of Eye Contact in Business Communication

Eye contact is an essential element of nonverbal communication especially in professional environments. Eye contact can communicate various feelings and messages. Additionally, is a crucial factor in creating trust, rapport and trust with colleagues as well as clients and other partners.

There are a few ways that eyes are a major factor in business communications:

Showing confidence and credibility In keeping and maintaining eye contact in talks and presentations will convey confidence, self-assurance and professionalism. It, in turn, will help you establish credibility and legitimacy to your viewers.

Building Rapport and Trust:

Eye contact with other people helps create a sense connections and understanding. This helps build relationships and trust within commercial relationships. It makes it much easier to collaborate or negotiate disputes.

Engaging the Listener:

Eye contact helps keep your listeners interested and attentive throughout conversations as well as presentation. Through eye contact your eyes show that you're truly interested in your listener's reaction and thoughts, thereby encouraging them to become more open to the message you are trying to convey.

Conveying Emotion and Empathy:

Eye contact is a great way to communicate emotions and show empathy which allows you to connect with people on a deeper and deeper level. By keeping eye contact even when you express compassion or understanding could increase the authenticity of your message and authentic.

Detecting Deception or Discomfort:

The patterns of eye contact will help you determine if you suspect someone is not being honest or feeling uncomfortable. The avoidance of eye contact, quick blinking or long-lasting stares may indicate insincerity, unease or disinterest. These can provide important insights into the person's mood or motivations.

Regulating Turn-Taking:

When speaking eye contact is utilized to indicate the need to speak, or to encourage participants to speak in the conversation, or to signal the speaker is finished the point. If you can use eye contact efficiently to facilitate conversations, you will have smoother and more efficient discussions.

It is crucial to recognize different cultural perspectives on practices of eye contact while dealing with individuals from different backgrounds. In certain cultures, eye contact is viewed as rude or unfriendly In other cultures eye contact is considered to be a mark of respect and honesty. Adjusting your eye contact manner to conform with the cultural norms could assist in maintaining effective communication the international workplace.

Analyzing Posture and Gestures

Power Poses and Confidence

Poses of power are postures that show confidence, authority and confidence. The power pose you choose to adopt will impact not only how other people consider you, but also the way you perceive your self. The research has proven that doing postures that increase testosterone levels, lower cortisol levels, as well as lead to a improvement in confidence.

Here are some powerful poses that can affect the way you communicate with your clients:

The Superman Pose:

With your shoulders apart, your hands resting in your hips, with chest and shoulders pumped out This pose is akin to the famous super-hero. This pose can help you feel more secure and relaxed, particularly prior to presentations or meetings.

The Victory Pose:

By raising your arms with your arms in an "V" shape above your head, this posture resembles the way athletes celebrate their triumphs. In this posture for a couple of minutes will help you feel more confident of achievement and confidence.

The Power Lean:

Leaning forward and placing your hands resting on a table or a desk during your speech demonstrates confidence and commitment. The posture can help your appearance more confident and confident in the course of meetings or during presentations.

The Leg Cross and Arm Rest:

As you sit by crossing your legs over the other while resting your arms upon the back of your chair oozes confidence and calm. The posture will help seem calm and relaxed in discussions or negotiations.

The Steeple:

The act of putting your fingertips in your palms a little apart, will create the "steeple" shape. This is a common gesture utilized by confident, top-ranking individuals, and it can indicate the authority of their words and show a level of thoughtfulness in conversations.

The Arms-Akimbo:

With your hands resting on your hips with your the elbows facing toward the outside, this posture conveys confidence and assertiveness. This pose can be especially useful when speaking to groups or expressing a message in discussions.

Although power poses may increase confidence and assert confidence, it's important to pay attention to what you do with the poses in various situations. If you are using power poses in the wrong way or use incorrectly can come across as intimidating or even aggressive. Find a way to balance the use of the poses in a controlled manner and mixing them with friendly, open body language that creates an engaging and positive impression in business communication.

Common Gestures and Their Meanings

Gestures play a vital role in the process of nonverbal communication. They can communicate a variety of implications. Recognizing the most basic gestures and the meanings they convey could help you comprehend the message others want to convey, and also enhance your communication abilities.

It is crucial to keep in mind that gestures' meanings may differ across different cultural backgrounds, so it is important to consider the cultural context before interpreting gestures.

Nodding and Shaking the Head:

The gesture of nodding typically indicates an understanding or agreement. approbation, whereas shaking the head from side to side indicates disagreement either disapproval or confusion. But, it can be different between different cultures like the one mentioned earlier.

The OK Sign:

The formation of a circle using only the index and thumb and extending the remaining three fingers is commonly considered an expression of appreciation or acceptance in a variety of Western societies. But, it could be considered offensive in some countries such as Brazil, Turkey, or Greece.

Thumbs Up and Thumbs Down:

A thumbs-up gesture indicates acceptance, approval, or appreciation, whereas the thumbs down gesture indicates rejection either in disagreement or disapproval. Take care when using this gesture because it could be considered insulting in some Middle Eastern countries.

The "Stop" or "Talk to the Hand" Gesture:

The gesture of spreading the palm by spreading fingers widely is a well-known sign to "stop" or "wait." However, in certain situations, the sign could be seen as disrespectful or rude.

Pointing:

Utilizing your index finger to point towards an object or person could indicate emphasis, direction or use to identify. Some cultures prohibit the act of pointing your finger directly at someone may be considered rude or even offensive.

Crossed Arms:

A person who folds their arms over the chest may indicate defense, resistance or rejection. The gesture could also suggest that someone is at a loss or is simply content at the moment.

Touching the Face:

The act of touching or rubbing your face, especially the mouth, nose or chin can signify an attitude of reluctance, uncertainty or uncomfortableness. It could also signal the deceit or stress.

Handshake:

Handshakes are a typical manner of greeting and acceptance across several Western societies. The force, length, and the style of handshake may convey various meanings including respect, confidence or even the feeling of friendliness.

Waving:

The gesture of raising the hand and then moving the hand side to side is a common gesture used to greet someone or say goodbye in many societies. The ferocity and intensity of the hand gesture convey various levels of excitement or a sense of familiarity.

If you are interpreting gestures, think about the context, as well as any visual or verbal clues to get a clearer comprehension of the message communicated. Also, being cognizant of differences between cultures regarding the meaning of gestures will assist you in avoiding confusion and make your communication more effective when working in different business environments.

Gestures to Avoid in Business Settings

Although gestures are a great way to emphasize your message, or even express your feelings, some gestures can be considered inappropriate or offensive when it comes to business particularly when you are dealing with those from different cultures background.

These are some hints to keep in mind when working:

The use of your Index Finger:

The act of pointing at something or someone using your index finger could be interpreted as unprofessional or even aggressive in a variety of societies. Use your hand open with the hand facing upwards in order to signal your direction or highlight a point.

## Chapter 2: Navigating Personal Space In Business Settings

Being able to manage personal space in professional settings is vital to efficient communication, creating relationships, and keeping business relationships. Here are some suggestions for controlling personal space in different professional settings:

Respect cultural differences Take note of customs, norms, and personal space habits when interacting with others who come from different backgrounds. Study and get familiar with customs and practices of various cultural traditions, and then modify your actions to show respect and tolerance.

Observe Nonverbal Cues:

Take note of the expressions of your body and the reactions of other people during conversation. If you notice someone is uncomfortable change the distance you stand at or your body's angle to make them feel comfortable. Be aware of signs of discomfort, like the crossed arms, the leaning away and avoiding eye contact.

Maintain Professional Boundaries:

Beware of entering into someone's private space when in professional situations, since it could be seen as incongruous or intrusive. Be sure to keep a distance between the social or personal zone when you talk to someone, and also take note of any physical contact such as kisses, handshakes, or pats on your back.

Utilize Space Strategically:

For presentations or meetings Use the space you have available in order to grab your audience's attention and help facilitate discussions. You can, for instance, either sit or stand at the center of the table in meetings or make use of the area at the side of the room while giving a presentation.

Be Mindful of Personal Space During Networking Events:

Events for networking often require having conversations with a variety of individuals in a short amount of time. Keep your personal space in mind and keep a safe distance between conversations so people feel comfortable.

Respect Privacy in Shared Spaces:

If you work in shared office space or in open workplaces Be considerate of other peoples private space and privacy. Listen to music using headphones. music. Avoid conversations that are loud as well as be mindful of your surroundings while moving about your office.

Be Flexible and Adaptable:

Prepare to alter your space preferences depending on your surroundings or the preferences of other people. Flexibility and flexibility with your style of communication can assist you in establishing connections and navigate a variety of workplaces efficiently.

If you can master the concept of personal space as well as proxemics within workplace settings, you will be able to make a pleasant and productive environment that encourages an open and collaborative environment and confidence. Understanding different cultures, paying attention to nonverbal signals, and ensuring that you are respecting professional boundaries are crucial aspects of being able to navigate your personal space successfully within the workplace.

Cultural Variations in Proxemics

Cultural differences play an important impact on the way the personal space and proxemics of people are seen and dealt with within different communities. Knowing these differences in culture is essential for efficient communication, especially when working in international settings.

Here are a few examples of how preferences regarding space can differ across different cultures:

High-Contact Cultures:

In cultures with high contact, for instance, those that are found throughout Latin America, the Middle East as well as Southern Europe, people tend to be closer during conversation and employ greater physical contact. In these societies, keeping the closer distance is considered an indicator of trust, warmth and friendship. It is essential to feel confident with greater distances as well as more physical contact when you interact with those from high-contact societies so that you don't appear indifferent or unfriendly.

Low-Contact Cultures:

People who live in low-contact societies, like the ones found in North America, Northern Europe as well as Asia tend to prefer having more privacy during interactions, and have less use of physical contact. In these communities, maintaining the distance between you and your partner is viewed as a sign of respect and professionalism. In interacting with those who are from cultures with low contact it is essential to observe the privacy of their space, and to avoid any physical contact.

Personal Space and Gender:

In some societies, people's spatial preferences can differ depending on gender. In certain Middle Eastern cultures, it is considered to be unacceptable for males and females to be close or even engage in physical touch in non-family relationship. It is essential to be aware of these rules and adapt your behaviour to reflect this.

Spatial Arrangements and Hierarchy:

In some societies the spatial arrangement of a space can reflect the social status or hierarchy of a person. For instance, in some Asian traditions, the center of the table, or the farthest seat away from the entrance could be reserved for the highest-ranking or respected member of the group. Pay attention to these habits and alter your seating arrangement or position to accommodate them.

Cultural Nuances in Gestures:

The gestures that are nonverbal can also differ in different cultures. Certain gestures can be considered inappropriate or offensive by certain communities. Pay attention to these variations and modify your manner of communicating to prevent misunderstandings and accidentally offenders to others.

In navigating personal space as well as proxyemics within international settings for business It is essential to stay aware of cultural differences and adjust your behaviour in a way that shows cultural sensitivity as well as respect. When you do this it will help you build better relationships, enhance communication and be able to navigate different professional settings with ease.

## Chapter 3: Reading And Using Vocal Cues

The Power of Tone and Pitch

Vocal cues, like the tone, pitch, as well as the volume, are important components of nonverbal communication. These could greatly affect the way your message is viewed in professional settings.

In gaining a better understanding of and utilizing the potential of vocal cues you will be able to communicate better express your emotions and thoughts as well as build trust with your fellows.

Tone:

Tone is a term that refers to the character of your voice. Your voice will convey feelings, attitude and motives. A friendly and warm tone will put people at ease and establish an environment of trust and trust, whereas the harsh or cold voice could appear hostile or insensitive. Paying attention to your tone helps you make an impression that is positive and encourage more effective communication between customers and colleagues.

Pitch:

Pitch is the term used to describe the tone or volume of your voice. It ranges from low to high. Higher pitches can evoke emotions of excitement, joy or even surprise. On the other hand, the lower pitch could appear formal, serious, or even calming. Take note of the frequency of your voice. Adjust the pitch according to the tone and message of your dialogue.

A few tips to use tones and pitches effectively for business use include:

Your tone and pitch should be matched according to the circumstances:

Adjust your voice depending on the setting and context of the discussion. As an example, you can use lower pitches and a more serious tone to give crucial feedback or addressing important issues, while a more pronounced tone and more energetic sound can be utilized to express excitement or celebrate successes.

Be aware of the cultural differences:

The different cultures have distinct expectations and norms regarding vocal signals. Be familiar with the ways of communicating vocally in those cultures that you're working with and alter your pitch and tone accordingly in order to show cultural understanding and reverence.

Control your volume:

A loud voice is often perceived as intimidating or threatening, and being too gentle could be perceived as unassuming or uneasy. Try to maintain a level which lets you hear clearly and not overwhelm the listener.

Practice active listening:

Take note of the tone, pitch and the volume of the speaker since these indicators can offer useful insight into their feelings and motives. Making sure you respond in a timely manner to these signals will improve your communication skills and build trust.

The development of vocal range:

The monotone voice can become dull and uninteresting, but a variety of vocal cues help keep the interest of your audience and communicate emotions better. Try incorporating a variety of vocal sounds into your speech by altering your tones, pitch and volume to be in tune with your audience and message.

Speaking Rate and Pauses

The pace at which you talk and your use of pauses within your words are vital aspects of your nonverbal communication. The vocal signals you use can affect the clearness of your message and the impression you make of your professionalism, and general effectiveness of your communication within business environments.

Speaking Rate:

Your speed of speaking communicate can impact the way your message is received. If you speak too fast, it can cause listeners to be unable to keep track of your thoughts. This may be perceived as a sign of anxiety or an absence of confidence. However slow speech can be thought of as a lack of interest or a lack of passion. Try to speak at a speed that allows the audience to absorb and comprehend the message clearly.

Pauses:

The use of pauses in a planned manner can improve your presentation by adding the opportunity for reflection, emphasis and giving a natural flow to the flow of your message. A well-planned pause are a great way to help your audience take in and retain information and also give you the chance to contemplate your ideas and keep your cool.

Here are some suggestions to use speaking speed and pauses to your advantage for business situations:

Your speaking speed should be adjusted for your target audience

Think about the level of familiarity of the audience to your topic and alter your pace according to their level of understanding. If you're speaking about complex or inaccessible facts, speaking at slow pace will help to ensure that your audience is able to comprehend.

Try to vary your speed of speaking:

Include changes to your speech pace to ensure that your audience is engaged and to emphasize important points. Slower speech can communicate significance or seriousness. Conversely, speedier paces can communicate the sense of urgency or excitement.

Pauses are a good strategy to take advantage of:

Pauses can be used to emphasise the most important aspects, to create tension, or give the audience to absorb details. The pauses give you an occasion to pause to keep your cool, and take a moment to think about your ideas when you are presenting or in conversation.

Do not use filler words or vocal pauses

The use of words that are filler, like "um," "like," or "you know," can distract from your message and can make you look less knowledgeable and confident. Try using quiet breaks to gather your thoughts and switch thoughts.

# Chapter 4: Building Rapport And Trust

Mirroring and Matching Body Language

Building trust and relationships among clients, employees as well as business partners is vital to achieving success in the business world. One effective method of achieving this is by mirroring and coordinating body language which is a subtle reflection of the messages of other people in order to build a rapport and show compassion.

Mirroring:

Mirroring refers to mimicking the body language, gestures and expressions of another. It can to create a feeling of understanding and trust, since it shows that you're at the same level and that you are in tune with their feelings and emotions.

Matching:

The term "matching" refers to the practice of taking a similar posture, the body posture, or stance with another. It creates a sense of alignment and harmony, showing that you're open to their opinions and the same space as their views.

Here are a few tips to effective mirroring and coordinating body language in order to establish trust and build rapport in professional settings:

Keep it simple:

Mirroring and matching must be carried out in a manner that is subtle and unassuming to avoid appearing fake or manipulated. Be aware of the person's movements and then make gradual changes to your own but without copying each move.

Focus on key gestures:

Look for the most prominent movements or postures that are being used by the other person and copy or mirror those. If, for instance, you notice that they're leaning slightly forward or leaning forward, you could also be leaning towards them to display the same level of engagement and enthusiasm.

Face expressions mirrors

The facial expressions that reflect the person you are talking to can to convey understanding and empathy. If they smile or smiling at you, smile to express your warmth and optimism.

Find a tone and speaking rate that match:

As well as the body language, think about being in tune with the speed of speaking as well as the tone and volume of the person you are talking to. It can help create a feeling of alignment and harmony the exchange.

Pay attention to cultural differences:

Culture-specific norms and expectations regarding body language may differ greatly and it's crucial to know the differences in mirroring and mirroring and. Learn about the nonverbal behavior of various culture and adjust your strategy to suit the needs of your culture.

Determine the answer:

Check the reaction of your partner to the mirroring you've done and match your attempts. If they appear to react positively, and then become more relaxed or enthusiastic keep using these strategies. If they seem uneasy or disengaged, think about altering your method.

The Art of Active Listening

It is an essential ability to build relationships and trust in corporate environments. This involves focusing fully on, observing and interacting with the other person's words, and demonstrating that you truly care about the thoughts and emotions of your listener. Active listening training can help increase your ability to communicate as well as improve the quality of your relationships and create a more cooperative and supportive workplace.

Here are the most important components of active listening as well as strategies to integrate these elements into your conversations:

Give your full attention:

Disconnect from distractions, like laptops or phones to concentrate solely upon the sound. Maintain eye contact, keep an open, receptive posture and try to avoid interruptions.

Be compassionate:

Show that you are able to comprehend and are concerned about the person's feelings and emotions. Utilize non-verbal and verbal signals for example, smiles, nodding or telling the speaker "I see" or "I understand," to show compassion and show support.

Review and

Review the speaker's key details in your own language to make sure you've been able to comprehend them. It can help to make the speaker to feel validated and heard.

You can ask open-ended, unanswered questions.

Let the speaker elaborate or clarify their ideas with open-ended questions for example "Can you tell me more about that?" Or "How did that make you feel?"

Beware of judgments or recommendations:

Try to understand the viewpoint of the speaker rather than offering suggestions or solutions. Avoid interrupting the conversation by offering your thoughts, opinions or advice If you are not specifically asked to do so.

Provide feedback:

Give constructive feedback or suggestions as needed, but always keep an eye on the speaker's thoughts and viewpoint. Make use of "I" statements, such as "I think" or "I feel," to convey your thoughts without placing your views on the speaker.

Be patient:

Let the speaker have the time to share their thoughts and feelings, without hurrying them or trying to fill in the silence. Be patient and allow the speaker time to speak in their own way.

Practice self-awareness:

Take note of your own attitudes, thoughts as well as your emotions throughout the exchange. It will allow you to remain clear and objective while focusing on the perspective of the speaker.

Projecting Confidence and Competence

When working in a professional setting, showing confidence and professionalism is vital to establish credibility, gaining confidence, and inspiring other people. When you effectively communicate these traits by your body language, voice, and behaviour and actions, you will leave an impact and create positive professional connections.

Here are a few suggestions for demonstrating confidence and competency within business environments:

Keep your posture in good shape:

Sit or stand straight, with your shoulders back and your head in a high position. An upright posture conveys confidence, self-assurance and professionalism.

Eye contact:

Make sure you maintain the eye contact of your conversations partners to show sincerity, attentiveness and confidence. Be mindful of differences in culture regarding eye contact and make adjustments accordingly.

Use purposeful gestures:

Use natural and well-controlled gestures to emphasise your points and show the energy and passion. Be careful not to fidget or make excessive gestures as this could signal anxiety or detract your audience from the message.

Be confident and clear:

Utilize a firm, consistent voice, with a clear pronunciation for a professional appearance and authority. Change your volume, tone and rate of speech according to the circumstances and your audience.

Wear professional attire

Pick clothes and accessories that demonstrate your competence, professionalism as well as the standards of the industry you work in and your corporate culture. Being well-dressed will not just create confidence, it also can boost your self-confidence.

Make sure you are prepared and know:

Be familiar with the subject of the issue, anticipate any questions or worries, and then prepare yourself to respond. Being prepared and knowledgeable can increase your confidence and proficiency.

Engage and listen to the other person:

Engage with others their thoughts and views through active listening, and asking questions with a thoughtful approach. Interacting with people through this manner shows confidence, skill and respect.

Maintain a positive attitude:

Be optimistic energy, enthusiasm, and an eagerness to make mistakes and learn from them. An optimistic attitude can give you confidence and grit even in the face of difficulties.

Be aware of the cultural differences:

Learn about the norms of communication, expectations and the etiquette that are prevalent in various cultural backgrounds to ensure you appear proficient and confident in a variety of situations.

Self-awareness, self-improvement and self-analysis:

Always evaluate your own strengths, weaknesses, as well as opportunities for improvement. Get feedback from your colleagues or mentors. You should also work in enhancing your skills and capabilities to show higher levels of confidence and competency as time passes.

# Effective Body Language in Presentations and Public Speaking

## 8.1. Planning and Practicing Your Presentation

For public speaking and presentations body language is an important role in communicating the message you want to convey, engaging the audience and showing confidence and proficiency. The right planning and preparation can aid in improving your voice, body language and overall presentation skills to ensure that you give an effective and memorable speech.

Here are some suggestions for making and preparing your presentation

Write your text:

The first step is to outline the major aspects and outline of your talk. Define your introduction clearly the key points, your main points, support arguments, and the conclusion. This will keep you focus and organised during the presentation.

Rehearse your speech:

Rehearse your speech many times in order to get familiar with the message and the timing. This can help you convey your message with more ease and with confidence.

Pay attention to body language

When practicing your communication, pay close focus on your body language, which includes movements, postures that are facial expressions, posture, and even eye contact. Create a set of deliberate actions and gestures that emphasise certain points and express passion.

Work on vocal delivery:

Be aware of your vocal cues like tonal, volume as well as pitch and the speed of your speech. Learn to modulate your voice in order to keep the attention of your audience as well as convey emotion. highlight important aspects.

Use visual aids effectively:

When using visual aids like props or slides, be sure that they support your message and make it easy for your audience to comprehend. Make sure you incorporate these elements in the presentation.

Do your practice on the mirror or make notes:

Doing your practice on mirrors or by recording yourself will help you to become more conscious of the body language you use as well as vocal cues. Check the recordings over and determine points for enhancement.

Get feedback from

Request family members, friends or colleagues for their comments on your presentation. Utilize their feedback to improve your presentation, and to address any concerns they may have.

Adjust to the changing environment:

Be familiar with the presentation room and presentation equipment before you start If you can. This can help you to feel more relaxed and secure during your presentation.

Find strategies to manage nerves:

Speaking in public can be stressful So, develop strategies for managing anxiety, like meditation, deep breathing exercises or self-talk that is positive.

Practice, practice, practice:

The more time you spend practicing you will become more comfortable and confident you'll become when presenting your talk. It is important to practice often in the days leading up to the presentation.

Interacting with the Audience by Your Body Language

Engaging your audience through an effective body language is vital for an effective performance or public speaking occasion. With the use of appropriate non-verbal cues it is possible to create rapport, maintain attention and deliver your message with greater effectiveness.

Here are some suggestions to engage your viewers with the body language you use:

## Chapter 5: Take A Calm And Confident Posture

Keep your shoulders straight with your head back, your feet spaced shoulder-width apart and your head up. The posture you choose to adopt conveys confidence trust, confidence, and self-assurance and makes your audience more open to the message you are trying to convey.

Keep your eyes on the ball:

Engage with your audience by making eyes contact with individuals while you talk. This creates a feeling of intimacy and shows that you truly care about the reactions of your audience and their feedback.

Use gestures purposefully:

Use natural and controlled movements to emphasise the most important aspects, communicate enthusiasm, and hold the attention of your audience. Do not use repetitive or ad hoc movements that could distract or indicate nervousness.

Alternate facial expressions

Make sure your facial expressions reflect the tone and substance of the message. Smile when you are able to communicate positive energy and warmth, or take a more serious approach in discussions of difficult or complex subjects.

Be sure to move with intention

Utilize movement to increase audience attention and reinforce key concepts. Move confidently around the stage or walk closer to the audience while speaking about key topics. Beware of a pacing and unfocused movement as they can cause distraction.

Keep your stance open:

Maintain your body language as open and attentive by looking at your audience while not crossing your arms. This creates confidence and encourages the audience to take notice of the message.

Pauses for use:

Include pauses in your presentation to allow your audience the chance to take in details, ask questions or just take a breath. The pauses will also allow you to highlight key elements and increase the an impact to the message.

Pay attention to your private space

Be respectful of your audience's privacy by keeping a reasonable distance, particularly when you move towards them. Be aware of differences in culture regarding personal space and adapt accordingly.

Monitor audience reactions:

Take note of the subtle signals that your audience may be sending out including gestures of the face, body language and levels of engagement. Modify your presentation, content and pacing as required to ensure that your audience is engaged and addresses issues.

Practice authenticity:

Make sure you are sincere and genuine in your presentation let your enthusiasm and excitement for your subject to be evident. A person who is authentic and engaging is much more likely to attract and hold the interest of his audience.

Handling Nervousness and Stage Fright

Stage fright and nervousness is a common problem for presenters as well as public presenters. Through developing strategies for managing the anxiety and build confidence you'll be able to give a more entertaining and effective talk.

Here are some helpful tips for dealing with nervousness and anxiety on stage:

Be well-prepared:

Prepare your material thoroughly and test your presentation several times. A good understanding of your content can help you build confidence as well as reduce your anxiety.

Prepare a presentation routine prior to the event:

Make a schedule to aid you in relaxing and focusing in the lead-up to the presentation. It could be as simple as deep breathing exercises, meditation methods, stretching techniques, or self-talk that is positive.

Concentrate on the message you want to convey, not on yourself.

Focus on the importance of the information that you're communicating and the effect the information will influence your readers instead of worry about how you're considered by others.

Re-frame your nerves as excitement:

Be aware that excitement and nervousness have a physiological connection. Be comfortable with your nerves in a way that shows passion and excitement in your chosen topic.

Engage with your target audience:

Engage your audience with eye contact, smile and be active with the people around you to build an impression of intimacy and trust. This can help to feel at ease and secure.

Grounding exercises:

If you are feeling overwhelmed or nervous in your presentation, calm yourself by paying attention to your breathing, placing your toes on the floor or by grabbing your podium.

Use positive affirmations:

Be reminded of your accomplishments, strengths, and skills. Positive affirmations can increase your confidence and ease anxiety.

Make sure you take your time:

Slow down, take deep breaths and stop whenever necessary to collect your thoughts. Keep in mind that you are the sole control of the speed of your talk.

Accept mistakes:

Accept that errors and mistakes are normal in public speaking. If you slip or fall on an idea, admit it, bounce back then move on.

Look for opportunities to learn:

The more time you've had when it comes to public speaking the more confident and confident you'll be. Find opportunities to practice speaking in the presence of other people, for example by taking part in a group for public speakers or assisting with speeches in your workplace.

## Body Language in Negotiations and Sales

### Identifying and Interpreting Buying Signals

In sales and negotiations it is essential to be able to discern and read buying signals from your client or prospect is essential. These are signals that don't speak that signal a person's curiosity and receptiveness or intent to make a decision or to make a purchase. When you recognize these signals you are able to alter your plan of action to increase your chances of success.

Here are some of the most common purchasing signals, and the best way to determine these signals:

Learning from:

If someone is leaning toward you in the course of conversation It could be a sign they're curious and engaged in the information you're offering.

Nodding:

A nod can indicate agreement with, understanding or even curiosity. If your potential customer's eyes are giggling when you present your proposal It's an indication that they're open to your offer.

Eye contact

Eye contact that is sustained may indicate that the individual is keen on your suggestion and is attentive to the message you're delivering. Be conscious of the differences in culture in eye contact, since the norms for making eye contact may differ between different cultures.

Mirroring:

If you notice that your potential client begins to imitate the way you move your body, like the way you move or your posture this could indicate trust as well as a positive relationship.

Expressions of facial expressions:

An authentic smile, or any other positive facial expressions like the crease of your eyebrows, or widened eyes are a sign of the interest and excitement for the offer you are making.

Legs or arms that are not crossed:

If someone does not cross their legs or arms during the course of conversation, it may be a sign that they're getting more open to the idea.

Asking questions:

If prospects are asking detailed questions concerning your offering, service or proposition is a sign that they're considering seriously the proposition.

Notes:

If your potential client keeps notes during your presentation, this could be a sign that they're interested and are keen to retain the details you've provided.

Care of the product

When selling in a sales situation, if a customer takes the time to examine, picks up or tests the product this is an obvious sign of an interest.

Discussion of specifics

If a prospect begins to discuss particular aspects, like price, delivery or the terms of a contract They are probably thinking about going forward with the contract.

If you spot some or all indicators of buying behavior you must respond in a timely manner. The best way to capitalize on the interest of your customers by offering additional details, responding to any questions and offering suggestions to any potential problems. Keep the rapport intact with your body language with a clear and positive communications. Be aware that every individual is different, as well as cultural variations can affect the way they communicate. Make sure to consider the context in which you are speaking and use your gut to determine the meaning of these signs.

Persuasive Body Language Techniques

In sales or negotiations using convincing techniques for body language helps you build confidence, build rapport and eventually, impact your client's or prospective buyer's choice-making process.

Here are a few effective methods to improve your body language and increase your persuasiveness

Maintain eye contact:

Eye contact can help establish an impression, shows confidence and proves that you're genuinely interested in the needs of your customer and worries. Be aware of differences between cultures with regards to eye contact practices.

Use open body language:

Relax your body and remain relaxed by sitting or standing in a straight position, with your arms free of cross-strain and looking directly at your prospective. The body language that is open signals accessibility and confidence.

Utilize purposeful gestures:

Utilize natural and controlled movements to highlight key elements communicate enthusiasm and convey your love about your service or product. Don't overuse gestures or use routine movements which can cause distraction.

Reflect your potential client's body language

Imitating your prospective client's facial expressions, like the way they move, their posture or facial expressions can assist in building rapport with them and help your prospect feel more comfortable.

Keep a calm and confident attitude:

Sit or stand tall while keeping your shoulders back and your head up, in order to show confidence, authority and expertise.

Smile genuinely:

A smile that is genuine can communicate the warmth, friendliness, as well as positive energy, which helps ensure that your prospective client is comfortable and build a more welcoming environment.

In a slight way, lean:

Engaging your potential client while talking can indicate the engagement of your prospect and show interest. This makes the prospect more likely to respond with your excitement.

Make adjustments to your vocal tone

Make sure you speak in a clear and assertive voice. Modify your voice to reflect your message's content and the emotion. your message. It will keep your prospects' interest as well as convey the enthusiasm you have for the offer.

Make sure to use pauses strategically:

Pause your speech to allow your listener to process information and also inquire about the information. The pauses will also allow you to highlight key elements and give an impact to the message.

Respect your personal space.

Take note of your potential client's privacy by keeping an appropriate distance throughout the discussion. Be aware of their non-verbal clues and adapt your approach in line with their needs.

Handling Objections and Resistance

In sales or negotiations managing objections and resistance successfully is vital to moving the conversation along and getting the desired outcome. Your body language plays an crucial role in how you handle and respond to resistance.

Here are some ways of making use of body language to confront oppositions and resist:

Be calm and collected:

If you are confronted with objections, keep your calm and collected manner. Maintain a relaxed posture keep your hands off the floor and breathe deeply to convey confidence and calm.

Make eye contact with your prospect Make eye contact with your prospective client in order to prove that you're attentive to their needs and ready to tackle them.

Use open body language:

Don't cross your arms and face the person you are talking to directly and keep a relaxed posture to show that you are open and willing to join in an engaging dialog.

Listen actively:

Make it clear that you're keen to understand your customer's issues by nodding, being a little more relaxed or using verbal cues for example "I see" or "I understand," to affirm the points they make.

Give your prospect space:

If the person you are talking to appears preoccupied or resentful, offer your prospect some breathing room by bending back slightly or stepping a little further back. It shows the respect they have for their space and may help ease tension.

Body language mirrors their reflection:

Simulate your prospects body language to build trust and build a relationship that makes it easy to respond to their concerns or concerns.

Make sure to maintain a positive voice

Utilize a calm, assertive tone when you address any objections adjust your voice in order to communicate the feeling of empathy and respect.

Utilize gestures to highlight your point:

Utilize deliberate, controlled movements to highlight your most important aspects and show your dedication to your potential customer's needs.

Let it be silent:

Allow your potential client time to take in the information and develop your thoughts. Allow some silence in your conversation. This shows you value their opinions and will be patient and wait for their reaction.

## Chapter 6: Show Genuine Warmth

Utilize warm and welcoming body language, like smiling and relaxed posture to foster an environment that is welcoming and supportive for your employees.

10.2. Reading and Responding to Team Dynamics

In your role as a manager or leader in the workplace, being aware and responsive to the dynamics of your team is essential to create a positive and harmonious work environment. In addition, nonverbal communication can give useful insights into the dynamics of your team and assist you in addressing all issues or issues.

Here are a few tips for interpreting and responding to team dynamics with body language

Be aware of group interactions

Take note of how members of the team communicate with each other when they are in meetings, discussion and other collaborative work. Watch for indicators of interaction and collaboration or tension including eyes, body posture and facial expressions.

Recognize non-verbal indicators of discomfort or disengagement.

Be aware of signs that the team members are feeling uneasy or disengaged. This could be seen as crossed arms or lack in eye contact or turning their backs on the speaker.

Be proactive about resolving conflicts:

If you observe non-verbal signals suggesting conflict or tension between teammates, resolve the problem promptly and in a constructive manner. Promote the openness of communication and listening to help resolve the issue and keep a positive working environment.

Encourage inclusion:

Be aware of your body language, which could accidentally restrict team members, or even create an illusion of authority. Make sure to use a positive body language and ensure eye contact with participants in discussion and meetings in order to create an atmosphere that's inclusive.

Adjust your style of communication

Change your body language, and communicate style according to the preference and preferences of the group members. It could involve reflecting their body language, altering your voice tone, or changing the speed of your the speech.

Encourage active participation:

Make use of body language with an open attitude like moving forward, and engaging in eye contact in order to encourage team members to engage in discussions and to share their ideas. Utilize positive reinforcement via both non-verbal and verbal signals such as smiling and nodding to recognize their efforts.

Pay attention to and deal with nonverbal indicators of burnout or stress:

Pay attention to signs of team members suffering from burnout or stress for example, slumped posture, fatigued expressions or the tendency to fidget. Be proactive and offer assistance, resources, or adjusting workloads and work expectations.

Make sure you use positive body language

Encourage positive body language in your organization, like making eye contact, indicating in agreement, or using non-judgmental gestures. This helps in creating a welcoming and cooperative setting.

Be aware of differences in culture:

Be aware that the body language standards can differ across cultures, and be mindful of differences when you interpret nonverbal signals from teammates with diverse backgrounds.

Give feedback and coach:

Provide constructive feedback and guidance to members of the team who may struggle with non-verbal communications skills. Aid them in developing their body language in order to increase their performance within the team.

Encouraging Open Communication and Collaboration

Collaboration and open communication between team members is crucial to a productive and successful working environment. As a leader, manager the way you conduct yourself plays crucial roles in encouraging the culture of openness and cooperation.

Here are some ideas on how to use body language in order to foster cooperation and open communication in your group:

Model open body language:

Show a friendly and open posture, for example looking directly at your team members and posing with a relaxed body as well as not crossing your legs and arms. It indicates your intention to speak up and work with the team.

Maintain eye contact:

Keep eyes when you speak or chatting with someone else. This shows your vigilance as well as your respect for their thoughts and views.

Use inclusive gestures:

Make use of gestures that encourage group members to join in discussion, for example hands that are open or arms extended. Beware of aggressive or exclusive gestures, which could hinder open dialogue.

In a slight way, lean:

Swaying slightly toward the speaker may signal enthusiasm and curiosity, which can encourage participants to discuss their ideas and thoughts more freely.

Encourage active listening:

Promote an active and attentive listening culture within your organization using nodding, paraphrasing and utilizing verbal signals to validate and acknowledge their ideas.

Take note of facial expressions

Your facial expressions should convey an openness, attention to detail, and a sense of empathy. Positive or neutral expressions will help to create an environment that promotes communication open.

Make use of mirroring techniques

Make sure you mimic the body speech of the team members in order to build the trust of your team members and to make your team members feel comfortable in sharing their ideas and thoughts.

Design a relaxing physical environment:

Place seating and meeting areas to encourage collaborative and open communication for example, setting up chairs in a circle or taking away physical barriers, such as big tables.

Pay attention and be present:

Let your colleagues know that you appreciate their contributions by staying present and engaged during meetings. Beware of multitasking, checking your smartphone, or pursuing other distractions.

Be aware of cultural differences:

Consider that body language standards can differ across cultures. You should adjust your language to show respect and acceptance of your team members with diverse backgrounds.

Detecting Deception in Business 11.1. Common Signs of Deception

Recognizing deceit in business settings can be a useful technique that allows you to make better informed choices and steer clear of potential traps. Although it is essential to be aware that there is no one sign of body language will be the sole sign of deceit There are a few common indicators that could indicate fraud.

Here are some typical signs of fraud to be looking for in workplaces:

Body language inconsistencies:

If someone is deceiving or deceitful, their body language might not be in line with their words. Be aware of any discrepancies between the words they're saying and body language, which includes facial expressions, gestures and poses.

Grooming gestures:

People who are deceived may make the gestures of grooming such as the hair, face or neck as an unconscious attempt to alleviate tension or anxiety.

Inattention to eye contact

The norms for eye contact can differ and avoid eye contact blinking excessively may be a sign of deceit in certain situations.

Micro-expressions are short, uncontrollable facial expressions that reveal the true feelings of a person, even if they're trying to cover their emotions. Watch for facial expressions that do not match their words or tone.

Gests that are in opposition:

False people may make different gestures. For example, shuffling their head "no" while saying "yes" or shaking their shoulders when making an assertive affirmation.

Fidgeting:

A heightened amount of fidgeting or nervous movement like tapping your feet or moving legs could indicate discomfort. It can also be an indication of deceit.

Modifications to speech patterns

The liar may show shifts in the patterns of speech like rapid pauses, stammering or an increase in usage in the use of words (e.g., "um," "uh," "you know").

Body language that is defensive:

People who are deceived may use defense-like body language for example, the arms crossed, bending their bodies away or even constructing physical barriers between them and other people.

Forced smiles

False smiles typically involve the muscles around the mouth, whereas real smiles work the eye muscles and also. Check for smiles that don't appear to be reaching the eyes, or look forced.

Uncertainty or excessive detail:

People who are deceived may offer excessive information to make their claims appear more convincing or deliberately vague in order to avoid getting accused of lying.

Assessing Verbal and Nonverbal Cues

In order to detect fraud when it comes to business you must be able to discern non-verbal and verbal clues. If you can determine the alignment with a person's speech and gestures, you'll be able to get a clearer picture of the truthfulness and motives of their actions.

Here are some guidelines to evaluate non-verbal and verbal indicators to spot deceit

Pay attention:

Be attentive to what the speaker is saying in his speech, looking for contradictions as well as contradictions and unclear answers. Watch out for variations in the speech pattern, like sudden pauses, the use of stammering or of fillers.

Pay attention to body language

Be aware of non-verbal signals which could indicate deceit for example, uncoordinated gestures, body language defensive such as forced smiles, forceful facial expressions or overly fidgeting. Be aware of the cultural distinctions and individual differences when you interpret the body language of your partner.

Be on the lookout for micro-expressions

Take note of brief uncontrollable facial expressions which could reveal the person's real feelings, even if they're trying to cover the truth. This can offer valuable insights about the authenticity of a speaker.

Assess the congruity:

Check the alignment of the words spoken by a person and their body expressions. Uncongruities between nonverbal and verbal indicators could indicate of deceit.

Establish a baseline:

Examine the person's typical behaviour and manner of speaking as they're relaxed and at ease. This can help you spot any deviations from the norm that could be a sign of deceit.

You can ask open-ended, unanswered questions.

Instruct the speaker to give more details by asking questions that are open to interpretation. This could make it more difficult for fakes to maintain their narrative and could expose the truth about their story.

Find the clusters of cues that are:

Avoid relying on a single cue to determine deception. Instead, you should look at a variety of verbal and nonverbal clues that indicate the presence of dishonesty.

Take care when interpreting:

Keep in mind that no one clue is an absolute indication of deceit. Be aware of context, personal variations, as well as cultural aspects in interpreting nonverbal and verbal signals.

## Chapter 7: Adapting Body Language For Remote And Virtual Communication

Adjusting Nonverbal Cues for Video Conferencing

As the use of remote work and communication, it's vital to adjust your body language in order to work in video conference environments.

Here are some suggestions for changing your non-verbal signals for clear and enjoyable communications during video calls:

Keep your posture in good shape:

Straighten your posture and stare at directly at the camera to show professional and confidence. A good posture will help to keep your attention on the right track throughout the conference call.

Use appropriate eye contact:

Focus on the camera while you speak to make a point of eyes with the people you are speaking to. This helps you create an emotional connection with your audience and show authenticity. If you are listening, take a look at the screen to demonstrate your appreciation, but do not stare in a long time.

You must frame yourself in a way that is properly

Check that your camera is set at an the eye level, and your body is in the frame. Your upper body must be visible and there should be some room above your head so that you don't appear tight.

Pay attention to expressions on your face:

The facial expressions of your face are evident on video calls So be mindful of how you express your emotions. Maintain your smile in a positive way to establish an atmosphere of positivity.

Use clear, concise gestures:

Hand gestures should be kept within the field of view, and try to make your gestures clear and concise. Extremely complicated or exaggerated hand gestures can be hard to read on a screens.

Beware of distractions:

Eliminate distractions within your space including the background noise, or any clutter so that your non-verbal messages are not disrupted or not understood correctly.

Wear professional attire

Although you might be remote, you must dress professionally for the meeting to show professionalism as well as respect to your coworkers.

Make sure you are using the correct vocal tone:

Be clear and speak with a consistent speed to ensure your message is heard. Pay attention to the tone and frequency of your voice because audio quality could occasionally distort your voice.

Make use of visual aids

In presenting your information, you should consider making use of visual aids, such as screen sharing or slides to show your point and to keep your audience interested.

Practice active listening:

Make it clear that you're engaged and alert by nodding your head smiling and by using affirmative words such as "yes" or "I see" as appropriate.

Building Trust and Rapport in Virtual Environments

Building trust and rapport in virtual settings can be a challenge because of the absence of physical presence, and the absence of non-verbal signals.

By following these tips, you'll be able to establish strong connections and encourage efficient communication even in remote environments:

Reliable and punctual:

Make sure you attend virtual meetings at the right time and adhere to the commitments you make. Reliable and consistent behavior can help you build trust with your coworkers.

Make sure you communicate clearly and succinctly

Make sure your message is easily understood and clear. Make use of simple language, stay clear of the use of jargon and give the context you require when needed. Clarity in communication prevents confusion and builds trust.

Stay active and responsive.

React quickly to emails and messages, and be active at virtual gatherings. Be aware and engaged in conversations by asking questions, offering feedback and recognizing others for their contributions.

Make use of the power of empathy and listening actively:

Be compassionate and considerate in your interactions with colleagues. Be attentive to their issues Ask follow-up questions and confirm their emotions in order to show your appreciation.

Share personal experiences:

Develop rapport through telling stories from your own life or experience that relate to the subject that you are discussing. It can make it easier to understand the online environment and help create relationships on an individual level.

Make your body language more expressive:

Keep eye contact, employ facial expressions and use appropriate gestures that convey your emotions and message efficiently. Take note of the different body language styles when interacting with colleagues from different countries.

Technology leverage:

Make use of video conferencing, text messaging, as well as other collaboration tools to increase the communication process and create a feeling of community. Make use of tools like screens sharing, digital backgrounds and break-out rooms to provide an engaging and interactive experience.

Encourage collaboration:

Create a more collaborative atmosphere through soliciting input, giving tasks to others, and promoting collaboration. Promoting a feeling of collaboration helps build trust and build trust between teammates.

Take your time and be flexible.

Know that virtual communications may be difficult, and there are technical problems could arise. Be flexible and patient and adapt to changes when needed.

Create a welcoming and positive setting:

Create a welcoming and positive setting by treating everyone with respect, recognizing the contributions of each person, and encouraging the openness of conversations. Honor team accomplishments and acknowledge individuals' achievements.

Maintaining Engagement and Presence Online

Maintaining the interest of your viewers and keeping a online presence can be difficult because of the inherent challenges of online interaction.

But, if you implement these strategies that you implement, you will be able to maintain your engagement and establish a captivating online presence

Make sure you are organized and prepared:

Make your virtual meetings and presentation in advance and ensure that you have the necessary items and tools in the right place. This can help keep a professional and focused manner of speaking.

Make use of multimedia and visuals:

Use visuals like slides, pictures, or video, in order to ensure that your viewers are engaged and reinforce your point of view. Visual aids can make a difference in the monotony of long-running virtual meetings. It also makes the content easier to access.

Engage and interact:

Engage participants by asking questions that are open to discussion, soliciting input from participants, as well as encouraging participants to share their ideas and opinions. This will create a stimulating and exciting event for everyone who is involved.

Make use of storytelling techniques

Involve your audience in the process by incorporating storytelling strategies in your talks or presentations. Stories make content more memorable and relatable keeping curiosity and focus.

Keep your energy up and keep yourself enthusiastic:

Show enthusiasm and energy in your body language and voice so that you can keep your audience interested. Be confident and clear in your speech and vary the tone make use of expressive gestures as well as facial expressions.

Create a comfortable environment:

Be sure your online area is clear of interruptions and background noise. Set the lighting, camera position and brightness for a professional, visually pleasing setting.

Flexibility and flexibility:

You should be prepared to modify the way you present your ideas based on your audiences' feedback and needs. You should be open to altering your plan of action or adding innovative ideas in order to keep your audience engaged and deal with any issues which may occur.

Maintain a personal relationship:

Inform your colleagues about personal experiences, ask questions about the experiences of your colleagues and show genuine interest about their wellbeing. It can build trust and build a more enjoyable and accessible virtual space.

Use breakout rooms as well as small-group discussion:

In the case of videoconferencing platforms make use of breakout rooms or small-group discussions for discussions that are more intimate and engaging. This helps maintain the engagement and enable participants to participate in a more active way.

Make sure to follow up and offer information:

Following your virtual conference or presentation, make sure you follow up with the attendees, providing them further resources, providing answers to their queries, or soliciting feedback. This shows your commitment to the success of your event and will help to keep the engagement going after the online conference.

The Path to Mastery

The Lifelong Journey of Mastering Body Language

Learning to master body language is a continual procedure that demands continuous education as well as self-awareness and practice. When you advance throughout your career and face various new challenges, improving your skills in non-verbal communication will remain vital.

Here are some suggestions for encouraging lifelong improvement in mastery of body language

Be open and curious.

Be open to a new perspective and realize that there's always room to improve. Keep an open mind to methods and new strategies for improving your non-verbal communications abilities.

Practice self-awareness:

Get a clear awareness of yourself by constantly reviewing your face expressions, body language and body language. Find areas in which you are successful and areas where you could use improvements.

Ask for feedback from people you trust:

Ask for feedback from friends, colleagues, mentors or your friends about your nonverbal abilities to communicate. Positive criticism could provide important information about areas you might need to concentrate on your work.

Learn and observe others:

Examine the body language used by effective communicators within your personal and professional daily. Examine their strategies and then adopt techniques that you can relate to.

Take part in training and workshops:

Take part in seminars, workshops or online courses that concentrate on body language as well as non-verbal communications. This can allow you to get new insight and develop your capabilities.

Explore books and articles

Be informed of the most recent advancements and research in body language through taking a look at articles, books and other materials. This can help you increase your understanding and keep up-to-date in the most effective practices.

Test and adjust:

Explore new methods or strategies and consider adjusting your strategy based on outcome. Be aware that what is effective for one scenario might not work in another. Be willing to change your approach to suit the changing circumstances.

Examine your performance

When you have important presentations, meetings, or meetings, take time to reflect on your behavior. Review your body language and reflect on the things that went well as well as what could have been improved.

Develop empathy and emotional intelligence

Enhance your capacity to comprehend and react to other people's emotional reactions, and your personal emotions. The ability to be emotionally intelligent is closely tied to effective nonverbal communication. It helps you deal with diverse social environments more effectively.

Keep at it and be patient:

The art of mastering body language requires some time and effort. Take your time while you strive to enhance your proficiency, and stay determined in your work.

Continuing Education and Resources

In order to keep and develop your body language abilities you must stay updated and keep learning. There are a variety of options and resources available that can help you improve your communication abilities that are non-verbal.

Here are some ideas for continuing education resources and courses:

Books:

Explore books about body speech, nonverbal communication and other related issues. Popular titles comprise "What Every Body is Saying" written by Joe Navarro, "The Definitive Book of Body Language" written by Allan as well as Barbara Pease, and "The Power of Body Language" written by Tonya Reiman.

Online courses:

You can enroll in online courses or webcasts that concentrate on communication, body language, as well as other topics related to them. Platforms such as Coursera, Udemy, and LinkedIn Learning offer courses taught by expert instructors in the area.

Seminars and workshops:

Take part in workshops, seminars or even conferences about body language and non-verbal communication. These types of events offer opportunities to gain hands-on experience, connect with experts, and keeping updated with current research and the most effective practices.

Professionals:

Be a part of professional associations like such as the Association for Business Communication or the International Association of Communication, that offer networks, resources and accessibility to events for the industry.

Mentoring and coaching:

Get one-on-one coaching and guidance from professionals who specialize on non-verbal communication and public speaking. A personalized approach will aid you with specific problems and provide you with a specific plan for developing your body language abilities.

TED Talks as well as other video resources:

Check out TED Talks as well as other videos about communications, body language and other related issues. They can give you information on the latest studies, developments and strategies and also provide actual examples of successful non-verbal communication.

Journals and research articles:

Be informed of the newest research into nonverbal communication by studying academic journals and articles. This will allow you to stay informed of the latest research results and increase your knowledge of body communication.

## Chapter 8: Convey Interest And Honesty

The personal space might be less than other European countries, so you should be well-prepared for more conversation.

Spain:

Spanish people typically stand up in close proximity during conversation, and have minimal physical contact.

Make sure to keep eye contact so that you show your sincerity and interest.

Make animated gestures to highlight the points or express emotion.

Mexico:

Mexicans can be seen standing closer in conversation, but they may also make physical contact.

Keep eye contact and convey interest and honesty.

Make use of expressive gestures with hands to highlight points and communicate feelings.

South Korea:

The bowing gesture is an accepted form of salutation and gesture of respect.

Beware of eye contact with directness since it can be perceived as threatening.

Be careful not to make gestures that are too loud, since the excessive use of gestures could be perceived as unprofessional.

Indonesia:

Handshakes are not uncommon, however, make sure to use a gentle touch, followed by the right hand placed over your heart.

Maintain moderate eye contact during conversations.

Make use of gestures with hands that demonstrate respect and politeness.

Turkey:

A strong handshake is a standard salutation.

Make sure you keep your eyes in contact with demonstrate trustworthiness and confidence.

Take note of any cultural or rituals of religion, for example never touching someone with the opposite gender outside of your close relatives.

Argentina:

Argentinians can be seen standing close to each other to each other during conversation, usually without physical contact.

Make sure you keep your eyes in contact so that you communicate sincerity and interest.

Utilize animated gestures to emphasise the points or express emotion.

South Africa:

Handshakes are an everyday occurrence and usually are accompanied by a smile.

Maintain moderate eye contact during conversations.

Utilize gestures of the hands to show respect and politeness.

Sweden:

Swedes value personal space, so maintain a comfortable distance during conversations.

Keep eye contact in order to demonstrate your sincerity and interest.

Make sure to use moderate gestures, and refrain from excessively expressing or obtrusive.

Netherlands:

Dutch individuals value their privacy and appreciate an appropriate distance when talking.

Keep eye contact with your partner on a regular basis, because it's considered an indication of integrity and reliability.

Make sure to use moderate gestures so as to avoid being too emotional or intrusive.

Switzerland:

Swiss people are adamant about privacy and would prefer the conversation at a distance.

Make sure you keep eye contact throughout the day for genuine interest.

Make sure to use moderate gestures, and refrain from excessively vocal or invasive.

Thailand:

Traditional Thai greeting is "wai," where you join your palms and make a slight bow.

Maintain moderate eye contact during conversations.

Make use of gestures with hands that demonstrate respect and politeness.

Vietnam:

The custom of bowing or nodding for greeting people from Vietnam.

Maintain a respectful distance during conversations.

Beware of eye contact, because it could be perceived as intimidating.

Philippines:

Filipinos can be more attentive when they talk compared to Western norms.

Make sure you keep your eyes on the ball to convey interest and honesty.

Utilize animated gestures to emphasise the points or express emotion.

Colombia:

Colombians can be seen standing close to each other to each other during conversation, and often do so without physical contact.

Make sure you keep your eyes in contact so that you show interest and genuineness.

Make use of expressive gestures with hands to highlight points and communicate emotion.

Greece:

Greeks tend to sit near to each other during conversation and employ touching to signal friendliness.

Keep eye contact and demonstrate interest and genuineness.

Make animated gestures to highlight areas and convey emotions.

Israel:

A strong handshake is a standard salutation.

Make sure you keep your eyes in contact with demonstrate trustworthiness and confidence.

Be aware of customs and cultural practices and make use of expressive gestures to highlight points or express feelings.

New Zealand:

Maintain a comfortable personal space during conversations.

Look at each other to display genuine interest and affection.

Employ gentle gestures in order to highlight the points, without being overly aggressive.

Denmark:

Danes appreciate privacy and like to keep the conversation at a distance.

Make sure to keep eye contact so that you show genuine interest and affection.

Be careful with your gestures and try to avoid becoming too expressive or intrusive.

Finland:

Finns prefer privacy and like to keep an appropriate distance when conversing.

Make sure you keep eye contact since it's seen as an indication of trust and honesty.

Make sure to use moderate gestures so as to avoid becoming too emotionally involved or intrusive.

Poland:

Poles may maintain a comfortable distance during conversations.

Keep eye contact in order to demonstrate genuine interest and affection.

Be careful with your gestures and try to avoid excessively loud or obtrusive.

Malaysia:

Handshakes are commonplace, however do not use a grip that is too strong, as well as the right hand placed over your heart.

Maintain moderate eye contact during conversations.

Utilize gestures of the hands to demonstrate respect and politeness.

Singapore:

Handshakes are a common way of making greetings to strangers in Singapore.

Maintain a respectful distance during conversations.

Do not make eye contact with your eyes because it could be perceived as threatening.

Egypt:

Handshakes that are firm are the most common way to greet people in Egypt.

Make sure you keep your eyes in contact with show confidence and trustworthiness.

Be aware of the cultural norms and employ expressive gestures in order to emphasise points and convey feelings.

Nigeria:

Handshakes are commonplace and usually is accompanied by a warm smile.

Maintain moderate eye contact during conversations.

Make use of gestures with hands that show respect and politeness.

Ireland:

Maintain a comfortable personal space during conversations.

Look at each other to display genuine interest and affection.

Employ gentle gestures in order to highlight your points without looking too aggressive.

Belgium:

Belgians respect their privacy and would prefer to keep an appropriate distance when conversing.

Keep eye contact in order to demonstrate genuine interest and affection.

Make sure to use moderate gestures, and refrain from becoming too expressive or intrusive.

## Chapter 9: Maintain Moderate Eye Contact During Conversation

Make use of gestures with hands that demonstrate respect and politeness.

Slovakia:

Slovaks appreciate privacy and would prefer to remain the conversation at a distance.

Keep eye contact in order to demonstrate genuine interest and affection.

Be careful with your gestures and try to avoid becoming too expressive or invasive.

Croatia:

Croatians appreciate privacy and would prefer to keep an appropriate distance when talking.

Make sure to keep eye contact so that you show your sincerity and interest.

Be careful with your gestures and try to avoid excessively verbose or disruptive.

Serbia:

Serbians may maintain a comfortable distance during conversations.

Keep eye contact in order to demonstrate your sincerity and interest.

Make sure to use moderate gestures, and refrain from becoming too expressive or invasive.

Bulgaria:

Bulgarians may maintain a comfortable distance during conversations.

Make sure to keep eye contact so that you show genuine interest and affection.

Be careful with your gestures and try to avoid becoming too expressive or invasive.

Estonia:

Estonians respect privacy and would prefer to maintain the conversation at a distance.

Keep eye contact in order to demonstrate your sincerity and interest.

Be careful with your gestures and try to avoid becoming too expressive or intrusive.

Latvia:

Latvians respect privacy and like to keep the conversation at a distance.

Keep eye contact in order to demonstrate genuine interest and affection.

Be careful with your gestures and try to avoid excessively expressive or intruding.

Lithuania:

Lithuanians appreciate privacy and like to keep the conversation at a distance.

Keep eye contact in order to demonstrate your sincerity and interest.

Be careful with your gestures, but avoid excessively expressive or invasive.

Slovenia:

Slovenians respect privacy and like to keep an appropriate distance when talking.

Make sure to keep eye contact so that you show your sincerity and interest.

Be careful with your gestures and try to avoid becoming too expressive or intrusive.

Uruguay:

Uruguayans can be seen standing close to each other in conversations, and often do so without physical contact.

Keep eye contact with your partner to communicate sincerity and interest.

Utilize expressive hand gestures to highlight points and communicate emotion.

Paraguay:

Paraguayans can be seen standing close to each other in conversations, usually by making light contact.

Make sure you keep your eyes in contact so that you communicate sincerity and interest.

Make use of expressive gestures with hands to emphasise points or convey emotion.

Costa Rica:

Costa Ricans might be more seated when they talk compared to Western norms.

Make sure you keep your eyes on the ball to convey interest and honesty.

Utilize animated gestures to emphasise areas and convey emotions.

Belarus:

Belarusians appreciate privacy and would prefer an appropriate distance when conversing.

Make sure to keep eye contact so that you show your sincerity and interest.

Be careful with your gestures and try to avoid becoming too expressive or intrusive.

Luxembourg:

Luxembourgers prefer privacy, and like to keep an appropriate distance when conversing.

Keep eye contact in order to demonstrate genuine interest and affection.

Make sure to use moderate gestures, and refrain from excessively expressive or intrusive.

Albania:

Albanians may maintain a comfortable distance during conversations.

Keep eye contact in order to demonstrate your sincerity and interest.

Be careful with your gestures and try to avoid becoming too exaggerated or intrusive.

Moldova:

Moldovans respect privacy and would prefer to remain the conversation at a distance.

Make sure to keep eye contact so that you show your sincerity and interest.

Make sure to use moderate gestures, and refrain from excessively explicit or invasive.

North Macedonia:

North Macedonians may maintain a comfortable distance during conversations.

Keep eye contact in order to demonstrate your sincerity and interest.

Make sure to use moderate gestures, and refrain from excessively personal or disruptive.

Austria:

Austrians usually greet each other with a firm handshake. They also keep their eyes on each other during the greeting.

When in formal settings, it's common to refer to titles and the last name when speaking to other people.

Austrians appreciate punctuality and it is essential to be punctual in attending any meetings or other events.

The respect for privacy is a must in Austria Therefore, avoid standing in close proximity to conversations.

Consistent eye contact is welcomed because it conveys credibility and honesty.

Hand gestures should be moderate so as to not appear emotionally or loud.

Bosnia and Herzegovina:

The people of Bosnia and Herzegovina can maintain a relaxed distance when conversing.

Make sure to keep eye contact so that you show your sincerity and interest.

Be careful with your gestures and try to avoid excessively dramatic or overly disruptive.

Georgia:

Georgians respect privacy and would prefer an appropriate distance when conversing.

Make sure to keep eye contact so that you show your sincerity and interest.

Make sure to use moderate gestures, and refrain from excessively expressive or invasive.

Armenia:

Armenians may maintain a comfortable distance during conversations.

Make sure to keep eye contact so that you show your sincerity and interest.

Make sure to use moderate gestures, and refrain from becoming too expressive or uninhibiting.

Azerbaijan:

Azeris appreciate privacy and like to maintain an appropriate distance when conversing.

Make sure to keep eye contact so that you show genuine interest and affection.

Make sure to use moderate gestures, and refrain from becoming too expressive or uninhibiting.

Kazakhstan:

Kazakhs may maintain a comfortable distance during conversations.

Keep eye contact in order to demonstrate your sincerity and interest.

Be careful with your gestures and try to avoid excessively demanding or interrupting.

Kyrgyzstan:

Kyrgyz people are adamant about privacy and would prefer the conversation at a distance.

Make sure to keep eye contact so that you show your sincerity and interest.

Be careful with your gestures and try to avoid excessively dramatic or disruptive.

Tajikistan:

Tajiks may maintain a comfortable distance during conversations.

Make sure to keep eye contact so that you show genuine interest and affection.

Make sure to use moderate gestures, and refrain from becoming too expressive or intrusive.

Turkmenistan:

Turkmen are people who value their privacy and like to keep an appropriate distance when talking.

Keep eye contact in order to demonstrate genuine interest and affection.

Make sure to use moderate gestures, and refrain from becoming too expressive or intruding.

Uzbekistan:

Uzbeks may maintain a comfortable distance during conversations.

Keep eye contact in order to demonstrate your sincerity and interest.

Make sure to use moderate gestures, and refrain from excessively engaging or demanding.

Cyprus:

Cypriots might stand near during discussions and may use physical contact to signal friendliness.

Make sure you keep your eyes on the ball to convey interest and honesty.

Utilize animated gestures to emphasise the points or express emotion.

# Chapter 10: The Power Of Nonverbal Communication

The use of nonverbal language, also referred to as body communication, is a potent technique that could greatly influence both our professional and personal lives. It includes all signals that we employ to transmit messages. These include facial expressions and tone of voice poses, gestures as well as eye contact. Research has shown that as much as 93% of all communication is non-verbal. This means it is crucial to comprehend the importance of our body language and the way it impacts the way we interact with people.

Understanding Nonverbal Communication

The first step in making use of the power of non-verbal communication is to be aware of the various kinds of nonverbal signals, and the way they interact to communicate significance. Below are a few of the most significant nonverbal signals as well as their significance:

Expressions on our faces: Our facial expressions communicate a variety of emotions, ranging from excitement and joy to anger and sadness. As an example, smiling may indicate warmth and affection, while the expression of a frown could indicate defiance.

Voice tone: The sound of the voice also communicates moods and feelings. As an example, a pleasant voice can signal enthusiasm and warmth, whereas an uninteresting voice could indicate the absence of enthusiasm or boredom.

Gestures: The use of gestures such as hand gestures, nodding and pointing may be used to highlight or reinforce the message we're trying convey. As an example, nodding could signify agreement, while the gesture of pointing could indicate an emphasis or direction.

The posture of our body is a sign of trust, authority, as well as the level of our interest. As an example, sitting up straight and looking directly at the camera will convey authority and confidence by avoid eye contact could be a sign of insecurity and lack of interest.

Contact with eyes: eye contact may communicate a variety of concepts, from excitement and attention to anger and dominance. In particular, maintaining eye contact throughout an exchange can indicate enthusiasm and interest, while not making eye contact could signal insecurity or disdain.

The Impact of Nonverbal Communication

Once we've mastered the many types of nonverbal clues, let's examine the effects they have in our interactions with other people.

First of all, the way we communicate will greatly impact how other people consider our appearance. In particular, if we are confident in our position and keep eye contact in a conversation people are more likely to think of us as reliable and confident. In contrast when we slump and avoid eye contact people are more likely to view our posture as untrustworthy or insecure.

Second, our non-verbal communications is a major factor in the results of the interactions we have. For instance, during the course of a job interview, using positive body language could assist us in making an impressive impression to the interviewer, and improve our odds of getting selected. In contrast, using a uneasy or nervous body language could reduce your chances of being employed.

The third reason is that nonverbal communication could significantly impact our relationship with other people. In particular the use of positive body language, such as keeping eye contact and smiling will help create trust and a relationships with other people. On the other hand, unkind body language, such as avoid eye contact and frowning could damage relationships, and cause others to be less inclined to believe our actions.

Tips for Using Nonverbal Communication Effectively

Once we've mastered the importance of nonverbal communication, we can discover some ways to use the technique effectively in our private as well as professional life.

First, pay attention to your body language. Take note of the way you look, your facial expressions and tone of voice and movements, and attempt to portray confidence, warmth and a sense of interest.

Second, pay attention to their body language. Take note of the way they look, their facial expressions, the tone of voice, as well as gestures in order to utilize these to determine their moods and attitude.

3. Use positive body language to create relationships and trust. Make eye contact or nod and make gestural gestures that show curiosity and commitment.

Don't use negative body language. Lastly should be avoided. Avoid body language that could damage your relationship with other people. It includes crossing your arms, staying clear of eyes, frowns and slumping. This can cause you to look defensive, distant and disinterested.

Fifthly, you should adapt your body language according to context. Certain situations require various body language. In the course of a job interview You may need to make use of an assertive body language in order to give the right impression. Likewise, when you are in a social situation one could make use of friendly body language in order in order to make friends with people.

Sixthly, practice active listening. It involves more than being attentive to what people are speaking, but also the way they speak. In this way it is possible to better comprehend their moods and emotions, and then respond in a manner which shows understanding and empathy.

Seventhly, you must be congruous in your body and language. Uncongruities between nonverbal and verbal messages can result in disorientation and even distrust. As an example, if you're talking about one thing and your body language suggests another message, people are less likely to believe you.

The bottom line is that nonverbal communication is an effective instrument that has the potential to greatly affect the way we live our lives, both professionally and personally. Through understanding the various kinds of nonverbal signals and the meanings behind them We can utilize the power of nonverbal communication to establish relationships, trust and positive relationships with people. Being aware of the body language we use and paying close attention to other their body language and employing positive body language regularly to improve the quality of our communication and increase the way we interact with people.

## Chapter 11: How To Interpret Facial Expressions And Gestures

Reading is the capacity to read and interpret non-verbal clues that provide insight into the thoughts, emotions and motives. It is a crucial skill for many areas of our lives such as relationships, business as well as personal growth. In this piece we'll explore how important it is to read individuals, the many kinds of nonverbal cues and some strategies to improve your ability to recognize people.

The Importance of Reading People

The ability to read others is an essential talent that can benefit in a variety of ways. In business, for instance the ability to read people will help to achieve better deals, develop better relationships with your clients or colleagues, as well as identify the possibility of problems prior to they become apparent. When it comes to private relationships, it may aid you in understanding your partner's feelings and desires, establish more intimate connections with families and friends, as well as deal with challenging social interactions.

Being able to discern the mood of the minds of others can serve as a useful tool for self-defense. If you are able to recognize dangers or threats using non-verbal cues it is possible to take action to safeguard yourself and prevent danger.

Types of Nonverbal Cues

The signal that people emit by their facial expressions, body language as well as tone of voice and other nonverbal actions. There are a variety of nonverbal signals that are important to be aware of in order to discern the personality of individuals:

Face expressions are one of the most expressive areas of the body. facial expressions are able to communicate a variety of emotions such as emotions like sadness, joy as well as anxiety. Common facial expressions are frowning, smiling, or eye movements.

Body language language is the method the body is used in order to communicate. This could include body posture, gestures as well as movements. For instance crossing arms could be an indication of defensiveness and leaning inwards can signal the desire to engage or interest.

Tone of voice tone and volume of voice is a way to convey feelings and feelings that cannot be conveyed by words. A humorous tone could convey an anger or irritability, whereas the calm, measured voice can signal confidence and a sense of control.

Eye contact Eye contact can be an effective nonverbal signal that could indicate curiosity and engagement or control. Eye contact is not always present. It can be a sign of dishonesty, shyness or lack of interest.

Tips for Improving Your Ability to Read People

Be attentive: The first step for discerning people's intentions is to watch their nonverbal signals carefully. Take note of movements, facial expressions and voice tone, and then try to figure out the message they're sending.

The context is important: Keep in mind that the meaning of nonverbal signals must be considered within the context of the context. For instance, a smile in a social setting could have a different meaning when compared to a smile at negotiations for business.

Learn empathy. Empathy is the ability to recognize and feel the emotions of another. When you practice empathy, it means that you'll be able to understand how you are feeling, and then respond in a manner that displays your concern.

Take note of your personal signals that are not verbal: Be aware your nonverbal behaviors influence how other people consider the person you are. Make sure you use positive body language like keeping eye contact as well as using gestures that are open, in order to build trust and establish relationships with other people.

Be aware of differences between cultures The way you communicate can differ significantly across culture. Be aware of differences in culture and be wary of making assumption based on one's own culture.

The ability to read people is an important talent that could assist you in a variety of areas in your daily life. Through understanding different kinds of nonverbal signals and focusing on the art of observation and empathy and improving your ability to understand people and develop stronger, deeper relationships. Be aware that all nonverbal signals should be considered according to the context, and different cultures have a huge impact in communication via non-verbal cues.

How to Interpret Facial Expressions and Gestures

The facial expressions and gestures we make are crucial nonverbal signals which can aid us in understanding and understand the feelings and motives of other people. Some studies suggest that 93% of the communication we do is non-verbal, including body language playing a major part in communicating meaning.

The ability to read the facial expressions and gestures of others can especially important in circumstances of social interaction, like discussions, job interviews as well as personal interactions. In this piece we'll explore a few typical facial expressions as well as gestures. We will also give tips on how to understand these.

Facial Expressions

Expressions of facial expressions play a crucial element of nonverbal communication because they provide crucial information about an individual's emotional attitude, state of mind, as well as attitude. Common facial expressions are:

Smiles: A smile is possibly the most widely-used expression of a face and is usually connected with positivity and happiness.

emotion. Yet, there are many fake smiles It is crucial to observe other signals like the appearance of crow's feet in the eyes to judge whether the smile you see is genuine or not.

The expression of frowning usually evokes negative feelings, like anger or sadness. A furrowed or sagging brow as well as a downturned mouth are common signs of frown.

The raised eyebrows or both of your eyebrows may signal disbelief or surprise. If it is combined with other signals like widened eyes or a mouth that is open raising eyebrows could be a sign of shock or fear.

Squinting: Squinting can indicate the presence of doubt, or suspicion, specifically when it is accompanied by the furrowed eyebrow. But, it could also indicate happiness when people smile when they're truly happy.

Lips that are purified: Lips with purplish lips could indicate discomfort or disapproval in particular when they are accompanied by the furrowed eyebrow. But, they can also represent the concentration of or a the ability to think.

Mouth open: A wide mouth may indicate shock in shock, excitement or shock. It can also signal anger or frustration if it is you notice clenched teeth, or a tight jaw.

Gestures

Gestures can be another crucial part of nonverbal communication. They are able to convey a variety of intentions and meanings. Some common gestures include:

Nodding: It is a standard gesture which may indicate agreement or understanding. But it can be an indication of frustration or boredom if used overly or in an unrelated manner.

Shaking your head: Shaking the head of a person from side to one side could indicate discontent or rejection. It could, however, signal insecurity or confusion.

It can be used to indicate an emphasis or direction, however it could also be perceived as confrontational or aggressive, particularly when it is done using fingers.

The act of crossing one's arms may indicate defensiveness, or the desire to establish the illusion of distance. It can be also a sign of peace or tranquility.

Fingers tapping: Tapping one's fingertips can signal impatience, or a sense of nervousness. But, it could also signal the excitement or anticipation.

Interpreting Facial Expressions and Gestures

The interpretation of facial expressions, gestures and movements can be difficult, especially since various people can use similar gestures and expressions for conveying distinct interpretations. There are however some general rules that will aid you in understanding nonverbal signals better:

Seek out clusters of cues A highly accurate ways to read nonverbal signals is to search for groups of signals that are pointing to an intent or feeling. As an example, if a person is frowning, crossing their arms and touching their fingertips, they could feel defensive or uneasy.

Be aware of the context. situation in which an facial gesture or expression occurs could give important clues to the purpose behind the nonverbal indication. If, for instance, someone is smiling in a job interview, it could indicate optimism and confidence, while when they smile during an intense conversation on an issue that is difficult this could be an indication of stress or an anxiety.

Be aware of cultural differences The different cultures could have different interpretations of specific facial expressions and gestures. In some societies, nodding can suggest disagreement instead of agree. It's important to stay conscious of the cultural differences and avoid making assumption based upon your own heritage.

Take into consideration individual differences. Different people express their feelings and motives exactly the same way. There are some people who are more expressive than others or they may deliberately conceal their feelings. It's important to take the individual's preferences into consideration when reading subtle signals.

Find the baseline behavior To accurately discern nonverbal signals It can be useful to identify a baseline of the typical behavior of a person. This will help you discern when someone's behavior is diverging from their usual patterns of conduct and is having a specific mood or have a particular intent.

Do not hesitate to ask clarifying questions: If you're not sure about the significance behind a gesture or facial expression It is always recommended to ask questions that clarify the meaning. This will help keep from confusions and leads to more clear communication.

Overall, the ability to discern facial expressions as well as gestures is a crucial ability in both personal and professional situations. When you look for patterns of clues, taking into account the context, paying close attention to individual and cultural variations, observing basic behaviors and clarifying questions, you'll be able to increase your capacity to correctly discern nonverbal signals and better communicate with your colleagues.

# Chapter 12: Mastering Your Own Body Language

The body language of a person is an essential aspect of communicating that could significantly influence how people perceive our appearance. If we can master our body language, we are able to communicate confidence, assertiveness and friendliness, among other characteristics. Here are a few tips to communicating the appropriate signals using the body language

Standing tall is one of the most important aspects of body language. being tall is a sign of confidence and confidence. Be sure to keep your shoulders relaxed with your head elevated and that your feet are spaced shoulder-width separated. Do not slouch or slump your shoulders to look unsecure or disinterested.

Make sure you keep eye contact can be a great means of showing the sense of security and attention. If you are talking to anyone, you should try to keep eye contact for a few minutes at a time nevertheless, you must be cautious not to look at or cause the person to feel uneasy.

Utilize body language that is open Use body language with openness. Open body language including crossed arms and legs, as well as a the relaxed posture can show the ability to be friendly and open. This is especially important in situations of social interaction or in trying to create trust with people.

Mirror the person's body language: Mirroring people's body language may aid in establishing trust and foster a feeling of connections. If, for instance, the person in front of you is leaning toward you, you may be inclined to lean forward too. Be careful not to do it too much or cause the person you are leaning against make them feel uneasy.

Make use of gestures to highlight your arguments: Gestures could be effective ways to make your points stand out and show excitement. As an example, you could make use of hand gestures to demonstrate the point, or even nod your head to express that you are in agreement.

Be careful not to fidget: Engaging in fidgeting or tapping your feet or fiddling with your hair could signal nervousness, or divert attention from the message you're trying to convey. Be sure to keep your eyes concentrated, and make use of gestures and other cues from your body to emphasise your point.

Pay attention to the facial expressions you use: Face movements can communicate a vast variety of emotions. Therefore, it's important to stay conscious of the message that we transmit with our facial expressions. A smile, for instance, is a sign of friendliness and openness and a grin can signal discontent or anger.

Be aware of the tone of your voice. The tone of your voice is an crucial aspect of communication, which is able to convey a range of feelings. With a calm and authoritative voice, you will demonstrate authority and confidence.

Pay attention to the privacy of your space. Your personal space is a crucial element of body language and we must keep an eye on how close we're standing or sitting in relation to other people. The general rule is that it's recommended to keep a distance of around three feet.

Keep your hygiene in check: Good hygiene is a key part of our body language and could affect the way others view our appearance. Be sure to dress for the occasion, and also practice proper grooming practices like brushing your teeth, combing your hair.

Learning to master our body language is a great way to communicate confidence, assertiveness, as well as accessibility. It is possible to send the appropriate signals, and be more effective in communicating with other people.

Chapter 4: Nonverbal Cues in Romantic Relationships

The love language is an issue that has captivated the public since the beginning of time. It is an emotion that is expressed in many ways and languages are one of the strongest instruments for communicating love. Through spoken words, body language or even actions in love, the language of love is a universal language which transcends boundaries, cultures or even the passage of the passage of time.

Today when communication is simpler and easier to access The language of love is taking on different forms and has evolved to adapt to our ever-changing world. Understanding how to speak the language of love will assist us in building better connections, communicate better, and communicate to those who whom we love.

Love is an incredibly multifaceted and intricate concept that extends beyond words. Other nonverbal signals like body language, tone voice and facial expressions can play an important part in the way we communicate affection and bond with our loved ones. In this piece we'll explore the role of nonverbal communication when it comes to relationship and discuss how recognizing these signals can enhance our relationship.

Body Language

The body language of a person is an effective nonverbal communication tool that can convey an array of feelings and intents. It includes every aspect of posture, hand gestures, to the physical contact of eyes and even touching. In intimate relationships the body language of a person is especially important since it can communicate our emotions and needs more effectively than words.

A major and important elements of body language that can be found when it comes to romantic relations is the physical contact. Research has proven that physical contact is an important element in romance, since it produces hormones, such as Oxytocin which help to build bonds and intimate relationships. Touch also communicates an array of emotions including love and affection to angry and frustrated.

Other cues in the body language which can play a role for romantic relations include the expressions of your face, eye contact as well as the posture. Eye contact, as an example is a sign of desire, interest, as well as affection. The absence of eye contact, on other hand, may indicate the opposite, namely disinterest or indignation. Face expressions, for example smiles or frowns, could convey a variety of emotions, ranging from joy to sorrow. The posture of a person can convey feelings and thoughts, with open and relaxed postures that suggest intimateness and comfort. On the other hand, tight and closed postures could indicate defensiveness or discomfort.

## Tone of Voice

Tone of voice is an additional crucial nonverbal signal when it comes to romantic relationships. How we talk in our voice, such as voice, volume, and speed, communicates an array of feelings and feelings. A soft and gentle voice may convey feelings of feelings of love and affection. On the other hand, an aggressive and loud voice can convey anger or discontent.

The tone of our voice may play a significant role in the resolution of disagreements in romantic relationships. What we say to the other person during arguments could affect the outcomes of the conversation. An amiable and calm tone will help defuse tensions and encourage constructive communication. Conversely, an aggressive and aggressive tone could cause the problem to get worse.

Recognizing and understanding the tone of voice used by our colleagues can enable us better communicate with them, and to respond to their needs emotionally. When we are attentive to how they talk to gain an understanding into their state of mind and react accordingly.

Facial Expressions

The facial expression is another crucial non-verbal signal in romantic relationship. They are able to convey a broad variety of emotions like joy, sadness or anger as well as fear. Recognizing and understanding our partner's facial expressions will allow us understand the state of their emotions and then respond to their emotions in the right way.

If, for instance, your partner appears sad or unhappy, we may utilize this data to inquire what they're experiencing and provide help or comfort. If our companion is happy or exuberant and happy, we could use this data to celebrate their happiness and rejoice together.

Expressions of facial expressions are crucial in communicating non-verbally in sex. Being aware of our partner's facial expressions as well as body language in a sex session can allow us better comprehend the pleasure they feel and how to respond to their desires.

Conclusion

Communication via nonverbal means is an essential element of relationships. Language, body language, the accents, and facial expressions provide a range of feelings and intentions which can be more reliable than the words. Recognizing and understanding these subtle signals can allow us connect better with our loved ones and to respond to their needs emotionally. If we are attentive to the body language of our partners and tone of voice as well as facial expressions it is possible to create stronger, more intimate relations based on trust acceptance, and respect.

## Chapter 13: Body Language For Negotiation And Sales

Sales and negotiations require more than the use of words. A large portion of communication happens via body communication. The research has proven that as high as 93% of the effectiveness of communication is non-verbal. That is that body language can be important in securing the deal.

Knowing how your body language is used in negotiations and sales can allow you to understand your clients' intentions as well as their emotions and respond to their needs. In this post we'll look at various signals that are used by the body to assist you to improve your sales and negotiation skills.

Eye Contact

Eye contact is a vital element of body language during negotiations and sales. It allows you to establish confidence and trust to the other party. If you're negotiating or selling something, it's important to keep eye contact in order to demonstrate that you're honest and reliable.

It is essential not to do too much. A prolonged eye contact could be perceived as infuriating or intimidating. Therefore, make sure to find a compromise between eye contact while turning away.

Facial Expressions

Face expressions can be a strong gauge of emotions. In negotiations or when selling it is important to be able to discern the tone of another's facial expressions in order to determine how they react to your words.

Smiles are a great approach to increase trust and create a positive connection with another. In contrast an expression of frowning or a frowning brow could indicate suspicion or disapproval. If you observe an unflattering facial expression It could be the right the right time to alter your attitude or alter your message.

Posture

Your posture speaks the confidence and your authority. Straight backs and an open position indicate you're comfortable and confident in your capabilities. The way you move your arms, or cross them may signal stress or defensiveness.

If you are selling or negotiating in any way, it is essential to keep a calm and open position to show that you are an authentic and reliable individual.

Hand Gestures

Hand gestures are often a good technique to emphasise an idea or to add more an emphasis to your message. But, it's essential not to do too much. Excessive hand movements or fidgeting are distracting and can signal nervousness or unease.

If you are using hand gestures, make sure they are organic and in a way that is specific. Examples include pointing at an item or making hand gestures to explain the feature could help to reinforce your point.

Mirroring

Mirroring refers to a method that allows you to match another individual's body language in order to establish trust and create a bond. In other words, if the person in front of you leans toward you, you could use the same gesture to indicate that you're actively active with the dialogue.

Mirroring helps create trust and help your partner feel more at ease with your reflection. But, it's crucial not to go overboard with it. A lot of mirroring could appear unsincere and manipulative.

Tone of Voice

Your voice's tone can communicate a lot about the way you feel and your intentions. A steady and calm tone could indicate confidence and stability, whereas the high pitch or shake of your tone can signal nervousness or a lack of confidence.

If you are selling or negotiating in any way, you must remain calm and in a consistent voice to convey your message efficiently. If you're feeling anxious or unsure, take time to collect your thoughts prior to proceeding.

Touch

The act of touching can be a potent method of establishing a relationship to the person you are with. Handshakes or pats on the back could convey gratitude and respect. It is, however, essential to exercise caution with touching.

Some people are not comfortable with physical contact. Therefore, it's crucial to pay attention to the signals of another person prior to making any contact. Also, you should be conscious of the cultural distinctions that could impact the suitability to engage in physical touch.

Proximity

The distance, or proximity between you and another individual, tells an entire message about the relationship. If you are selling or negotiating it is essential to maintain a certain distance in order to build a relationship with your counterpart. Being too close to someone could be perceived as intrusive or aggressive. Standing too far can signify an absence of interest or lack of commitment.

The ideal distance can differ dependent on the specific situation as well as the norms that are prevailing among both parties. It is generally recommended to follow each other's distance in order to create a safe distance between the two the parties.

Micro-expressions

Micro-expressions are facial expressions that are short that reveal someone's emotion, even when they're trying to cover the truth. They can be as small as one-half of a second which makes them hard to recognize without practice.

A few common micro-expressions are an occasional raise of the eyebrows, pursing of the lips or tightening of the jaw. If you can learn to discern micro-expressions you will get a better understanding of the of the other's emotions and thoughts and allow you to alter your behavior accordingly.

Listening Skills

Listening is an essential aspect of effective communication. the body language plays an important part in the listening process. While listening, it's essential to remain focused and refrain from distracting actions such as fidgeting, or glancing away.

Furthermore, a smile or signs that don't speak can signal you're engaged and paying attention to your partner. Through effective listening as well as paying attention to of the other's body language it will give you a better comprehension of their wants and worries, which will allow you to customize your approach and improve the chances of a successful negotiation purchase.

Conclusion

Body language is a vital aspect of sales and negotiation. Through understanding and utilizing the body language effectively it will help you increase your ability to communicate to build trust and improve your odds of successfully closing deals.

A few key cues for body language to remember includes keeping eye contact and reading facial expressions being confident and open posture. This is done by making deliberate hand gestures and mirroring of the other's body language by using a appropriate tone of voice. Also, it is important to be conscious of contact and closeness, as well as knowing how to interpret the micro-expressions.

Good listening skills are important, because they help you to comprehend the person's requirements and needs and concerns, then tailor your strategies to meet their needs. When you incorporate these signals from your body in your sales and negotiation strategies, you will increase your skills in communication and improve your odds for success.

## Chapter 14: Conquering Public Speaking

Public Speaking

Public speaking is the art of making a speech, or even a presentation before an audience in person. It's a ability that is developed through training and practice, and is crucial to a variety of professional and personal occasions such as business talks as well as academic lectures and occasions for the public.

Effective public speaking involves an array of verbal as well as nonverbal communication abilities. Beyond the actual content in the presentation, the body speech, voice tone and the delivery style significantly affect the way in which the message is received by the listeners.

Here are a few key points for enhancing your public speaking abilities:

Know your audience

In the beginning of delivering your talk or giving a speech It is crucial to think about who your audience and what their preferences and desires are. This allows you to adapt your speech and presentation manner to make it more appealing and pertinent to your people who will be watching.

Practice and practise, practice

The practice of speaking is crucial to improving the skills of public speaking. Practice your presentation or speech will help you become more comfortable and confident in your presentation, which allows you to be more focused on the way you communicate your message.

Use effective body language

The way you present yourself can have a huge impact on the way your message is perceived by your people who are watching. Maintaining eye contact while using deliberate hand gestures, as well as maintaining a good posture will make you appear more enthused and confident.

Be confident and clear in your speech.

Confidently and clearly speaking is essential to convey your message clearly. You should slow down your pace make sure you use the correct intonation and inflection. You can also vary the pitch and volume to keep your audience interested.

Make use of visually-based tools

Visual aids, including props or slides, could aid in enhancing your presentation and help make it memorable for your audience. Be careful not to put too much emphasis using visual aids since they could be distracting when they are used too often.

Engage with the viewers

Engaging your audience will help keep them engaged and focused through your talk or presentation. You can do this by engaging the audience with questions, utilizing humorous remarks, or by giving personal stories or experiences that pertain to the subject.

Be ready for the possibility of being asked questions.

Make sure you are prepared to address the questions of your audience members at the conclusion of your speech or the presentation. This will aid in clarifying your message, and demonstrate that you have a thorough understanding of your subject.

As well as these guidelines It is also important to be aware the fact that speaking in public is an art which can be honed and improved through repetition. Do not be afraid to ask opinions from other people as you work in enhancing your manner and your message.

In the end, public speaking is an essential talent that could greatly enhance the development of your career and personal life. Utilizing effective communication strategies and regularly practicing it is possible to develop into an experienced and captivating presenter who is able to captivate and motivate the public.

Speaking in public can be an intimidating experience for many people, however it's an ability that can be learned through practice and training. The most important aspect to effective public speaking involves using the body language to enhance your ability to present. In this piece we'll explore ways the body language you use can improve your presentation skills and offer guidelines for how to use it effectively.

Why is Body Language Important in Public Speaking?

Body language is the term used to describe the signals that are non-verbal to express our feelings, thoughts, and moods. They can consist of hands, facial expressions or postures, as well as eye contact among other things. When speaking in public it is vital to use body language as it has a significant impact on the way your message is perceived by your audience.

Utilizing appropriate body language will assist you in appearing more confident, positive and convincing, whereas employing negative body language may hinder your presentation and appear tense or inexperienced.

Tips for Using Body Language in Public Speaking

Get started with a posture that is good

A good posture is essential in establishing confidence and power. Keep your posture straight and by putting your shoulders back, and your chest up. Do not slouch or lean onto one side, as that can look indifferent or inexperienced.

Maintain eye contact

Eye contact with your people in the audience is a crucial part of delivering a professional public speech. This shows you're in contact with your audience and confidence in the message you are delivering. Be sure to avoid looking at one individual all the time, since they may feel uncomfortable. Be sure to make eye contact with people in the crowd.

Make sure you use hand gestures that are purposeful.

Hand gestures can be used to highlight your message, and help your appearance more appealing with your audience. Make use of hand gestures that are purposeful to emphasize key ideas or highlight important concepts. Do not use too many gestural gestures as they could cause distraction or distract from your point.

Utilize facial expressions to convey emotions

Face expressions are an effective way of conveying emotion as well as highlighting important points within your talk. Utilize facial expressions in order to demonstrate passion, interest and enthusiasm for your subject. Be careful not to be overly extreme or exaggerated facial expressions, because this may cause you to look unprofessional or insincere.

Utilize movement to keep your viewers interested.

Moving your body can be a great means to keep the crowd engaged and engaged during your presentation. Moving around on stage, or use gestures to signal the movement or changes. Be careful not to move fast or for too long since this may become distracting or even detract from the message.

Utilize the right tone and volume

The volume and tone of your voice will greatly affect the way your message is perceived by the public. Make sure you use a tone and volume that are right for your message and the audience. Be confident and clear and avoid filler words such as "um" or "uh" which can distract from the message.

Mirror the public

The body language of the audience will help build rapport and create a rapport to the audience. Take note of your audience's face expressions, postures, and voice tone, as well as adjusting your body language to be in line with the audience's. This will help to build a sense and connection between the two of you.

Visual aids can help you convey the message

Visual aids, including the use of props or slides can help improve your presentation to make it more memorable for your audience. Make use of visual aids only sparingly but ensure that they're relevant and contribute value to the presentation.

Conclusion

Effectively using body language is essential to public talking. Through a proper posture, keeping eye contact and using deliberate hand gestures, using the right tones and volumes, and mimicking the body language of your audience and tone, you will be able to improve your communication and make yourself appear more confident and engaging your audience.

Keep in mind the importance of body language. It is only an aspect in the art of public speaking. Training and practice are crucial to delivering the best speech or a presentation. Through combining these components and practice, you will be a better public speaker, and reach your objectives.

It's crucial to understand the art of mastering your body language public speaking requires perseverance and training. It's not something you is easy to master in a single day as it takes an effort on your part to get better. Another way to practice the body language you use is to film yourself doing your presentation or speech and review it to determine the areas you could enhance your performance.

In addition, getting opinions from others could prove beneficial. Request a colleague or a friend to observe you as you speak and offer comments on how you are using the way you speak. They may offer suggestions for ways to improve your performance and also offer support while you work to improve your public speaking abilities.

Effectively using body language will greatly improve the effectiveness of your public speaking and assist you in becoming an engaging and convincing public speaker.

Through practicing a proper posture, keeping eye contact using deliberate hand gestures, utilizing appropriate volumes and tone, mirrored to the audience's movements as well as visual aids, you will improve your performance as a public speaker, and reach your objectives. Make sure to practice and plan as well, and never be afraid to get feedback from others and keep improving and becoming the speaker.

## Chapter 15: Navigating Different Cultures

Globalization has made intercultural communication has become ever more crucial. In different cultures, there are diverse customs, practices and communication methods. Knowing and understanding these different cultures is vital to establishing effective communicating and establishing connections.

The body language plays an important function in the cross-cultural exchange. It's a universal communication method which can transmit a large amount of information, without the need of words. The interpretations of body language may differ widely across culture, and what's acceptable in one society might not apply to the other.

For a successful way to navigate across cultures It is important to know the subtleties of body language used in every different culture. Here are some suggestions to use body language when it comes to intercultural communications:

Study the culture before embarking on a cross-cultural conversation conduct some background research about the people you'll interact with. Discover the customs, practices and methods of communication. It will allow you to not accidentally offend or confuse their customs, traditions and ways of communicating with them.

Pay attention to the personal space of yours: The space between you and others is different across culture. Certain cultures have individuals are more closely grouped during conversations, whereas some prefer to be further apart. Take note of this and change your distance accordingly.

Be aware of eye contact. This is yet another aspect that can cause cultural discord. For some people it is considered to be an indication of engagement and respect however in other cultures, it could be considered hostile or even disrespectful. Be aware of the culture practices and adapt accordingly.

Learn to recognize how to use hand gestures may differ across different the different cultures. A few gestures that seem perfectly accepted in one society may be considered offensive to another. Like, for instance"OK" sign "OK" sign may be considered a positive sign within the United States, but it may be seen as offensive in other nations.

Pay attention to your posture. This is a key element of body language, and it may differ across different cultural backgrounds. For some people, sitting down and crossing the legs can be considered disrespectful however in other cultures the situation, it is completely acceptable.

Utilize facial expressions: Face expressions are a different aspect of body communication. But, how we interpret facial expressions can differ among the different cultures. A smile, for instance, can be seen differently in various cultural contexts. In certain cultures smiles are viewed as a sign of courtesy and in some the same way, it could be interpreted as a sign of insincerity.

Be patient and flexible Also, remain sensitive and flexible while dealing with diverse cultural differences. It can take a while to grasp the intricacies of body language when you are in the new language, and it is possible to make mistakes on the process. If you're willing and open to constructive feedback, you'll be able to enhance your cross-cultural communication abilities as time passes.

## Chapter 16: The Dark Side Of Body Language

The body language is a potent tool to communicate However, it also can be used to conceal information and manipulating. Recognizing the signs that an individual is using the body language of a person to trick or manipulate others is a crucial skill to have in professional and private contexts.

There are a variety of body language signs that are used to deceive and manipulate. This includes:

Refraining from eye contact: Those who are deceiving or seeking to influence are often hesitant about engaging in eyes contact with each other. They might look away or downwards, or could employ different strategies for avoiding eye contact like wearing glasses or concealing behind an cap.

Covering or touching the face Covering or touching the face: People who are lying or manipulating might cover or touch their faces as a means to hide their feelings or avoid eye contact. It is also possible to put their fingers on or over their mouths or ear, which could be an indication that they're not sincere.

Fidgeting, or fiddling with objects people who lie or attempting to manipulate objects may be seen fiddling with objects to aid in relaxing anxiety or stress. It is possible to play with hair, play with the pen or swipe their hands as a method to distract themselves from discussion.

Body language that is inconsistent: When somebody is lying or attempting to deceive the body language of another, it could differ from the message they're trying to convey. As an example, they might smile to show acceptance, however the body language of their expression suggests they're actually not agreeing.

Closed body language: Those who lie or are trying to trick others might use closed body language, for example moving their arms or legs in the hope of making a wall between them with the person they are trying to manipulate.

It is important to remember that body language signs don't always indicate of deceit or manipulation. Eye contact is not always a good thing. or twitch with objects due to numerous reasons. However, it's crucial to think about the context along with other variables in interpreting the body language signals.

If the body language signals are coupled with other indicators of manipulation or deceit, like inconsistencies in their narrative or an epoch of deceitful behavior They could provide a clear indication that something isn't right.

What can you do to safeguard yourself from being manipulated and tricked via your body speech?

Take note of your body language Be conscious of typical body language signals that are that are associated with manipulation and deceit

You can become more aware of these actions when they are observed.

Check for contradictions: If somebody is lying or attempting to influence others, their body language could not be in line with the words they're telling you. Check for differences between what they say and body language in order to decide if they're honest.

Take into consideration the context: It is important to take into consideration the environment and the other variables in the interpretation of body language. As an example, a person who normally is fidgety might not be deceiving solely because they're tapping their feet.

Be awestruck by your intuition If you feel something is strange, it's likely to be. Be awed by your intuition and make sure you protect yourself against any possible deceit or manipulative behavior.

It's important to keep in mind that although body language could be an effective tool in detection of manipulation and deceit however it shouldn't be the only element in the determination of someone's integrity or credibility. Other elements, including previous behavior as well as the context of the circumstance, should be considered as well.

The bottom line is that body language is a potent means of communication, however it also can be utilized to deceive and manipulate. If you are aware of the common signs of body language used for manipulation and deceit and also by examining the context as well as other aspects that can help you be protected from any harm that could come your way. Be aware of your own instincts and if you notice something that isn't right make sure you protect yourself.

Putting it All Together: Integrating Nonverbal and Verbal Communication for Maximum Impact

Effective communication requires not only nonverbal but also verbal aspects, and the integration of the two can significantly impact the efficacy in your communication. If you pay attention to your non-verbal and spoken messages, you'll be able to create an even more compelling and powerful message that is resonant with your target audience.

Here are some suggestions for integrating verbal and nonverbal communications to maximize impact

Take note of the way you present yourself: Your body language will communicate an important message about you and the level of trust you have. Take note of your hand movements, posture as well as facial expressions and make sure that they correspond to the message you're trying to communicate.

Make use of hand gestures to highlight the most important aspects: Hand gestures are an effective way of highlighting the most important aspects of your message. Utilize gestures that come naturally for you and be sure they're on par with the message you're saying.

Create eye contact Eye contact: Eye contact is an essential part of non-verbal communication and can be a great way to connect to your viewers. Eye contact is important with people who are in the crowd Try to keep for only a few seconds.

Make use of facial expressions to communicate emotion. Your facial expressions will convey what you think about the message you are sending. Utilize facial expressions to express emotion, excitement and conviction in the message you are trying to convey.

Take note of your voice tone A tone of voice will also communicate a lot about the message you are trying to convey and also your feelings. Be sure that your tone of voice matches the message you are trying to convey, and also attempt to alter your tone to keep your audience interested.

Learn to practice active listening. The act of listening is not just listening to what someone else is speaking and being aware of their body language as well as accent. When you practice active listening will help you better comprehend your target audience and customize your messages to meet their requirements.

Being authentic is essential to the effectiveness of communication. Let your personality shine through and let your individuality reflect in your verbal as well as non-verbal communication. This can help you communicate with your customers on a more of a degree.

When you combine nonverbal and verbal communications, you will be able to create an effective and powerful message that is resonant with your viewers. When you're conducting a presentation, engaging in conversations, or giving your speech, paying close attentively to your nonverbal and verbal communication will help you convey your message more effectively and get your goal.

## Chapter 17: The Foundations Of Nonverbal Communication

A. The foundations of nonverbal communications

1. Micro expressions and looks

The role of ooks is significant in communicating emotions and goals. In this section, we explore the many kinds of eyes and the significance they play in establishing a relationship. From genuine smiles to wrinkled eyes Every expression conveys an important signal. This article will explore the physics behind micro expressions that are short essential facial expressions which can reveal real feelings even when people are trying to conceal the truth. If you can identify it and interpret the facial expressions precisely, you can get valuable insight of the emotions and thoughts of other people.

2. Hand movements and motions

Hand movements and gestures provide depth and meaning to the words we speak. They may highlight central themes as well as convey enthusiasm or signal that we are in agreement. In this section, we examine the many kinds of gestures as well as their contexts. The range of gestures can be anything from a sign of trust and openness, to closed or stoic stances and more, we'll look into the ways that different movements of hands influence the way how others perceive us. Knowing how to use signals can assist in improving your communication and interacting with people effectively.

3-Stance as well as body positioning

Pose is one of the most important components of non-verbal communication. It can communicate authority, certainty and even a sense of acceptance. In this section we'll discuss the significance of body posture and the way it affects how others perceive you. The focus will be on the differences between closed and open postures of the body and what effect on the relationship elements. Additionally, we will delve into the concept of force postures, and the ways in which adopting specific body postures will help you to be more confident and affect in a variety of situations.

## Chapter 18: Understanding The Role Of The Eye-To-Eye

Eye to eye contact is a powerful non-verbal indicator which can establish the foundation for trust, connection and awareness. This section will examine the importance of eye to eye connections in the context of the context of correspondence. It will look at the relevant and social variables that affect eye to eye connectivity and design. In addition, we'll look at the different kinds of appearances such as social or private style, as well as professional look. You will be able to understand the ways they convey different messages and objectives. Being a master of eye-to-eye contact can help you build solid relationships and show the real passion and enthusiasm.

C. Resonance in vocal sounds and its impact on non-verbal communications

Non-verbal communication primarily consists of the use of non-verbal communication, vocal resonance also plays an important role in the process of correspondence. In this article we'll examine how the tone of your voice or pitch could affect the message communicated. The focus will be on the concept of compatibility between your voice and other sounds, in which your speech style is in line with your non-verbal signals, thereby increasing the credibility and legitimacy of your speech. Knowing the relationship between the resonance of your voice and non-verbal communication can help you communicate more effectively and communicate the intended meaning of your speech.

If you master the basics of nonverbal communication, such as gestures, signs eye-to-eye contact, and vocal resonance, you'll build a solid foundation for knowing and using nonverbal communications to benefit yourself. These fundamental standards serve as the building blocks of building your moxy and impacting other people, and eradicating the power of non-verbal communication.

III. How to dominate your own Non-verbal Communication

A. Making awareness

1. Inspecting and distinguishing the apprehensive characteristics

The most important thing is to be indulgent. It's the first step towards ensuring that you control the non-verbal communications. In this section we'll look at common indifferences that could ruin the effectiveness of your communication. For instance squirming, nail-gnawing or avoiding eye-to-eye contact. It will help you to spot these tendencies for yourself, and discover the root causes. The course will provide down-to the earth methods and strategies for observing and reducing the tense ways you behave that allow you to display confidence and be in control of all situations.

## Chapter 19: Strong Correspondence

Eye to eye connections are the most important tools for effective communication. In this section we'll dive into the nuances of using the eyes and connection in order to effectively transmit your message in a more effective manner. Learn the best way to adapt your appearance with your communication to ensure authenticity and compatibility. There will be strategies to staying in contact, which builds relationships and trust as well as adapting to personal preferences and social norms. If you can dominate these views and focusing on these, you'll end up becoming a charming communicator who will attract and influence people through non-verbal signals.

Focusing on creating consciousness, building a solid non-verbal communication skills, improving non-verbal appearance, and using the eye and eye connections, you'll gain control over your own non-verbal communications. This will allow the ability to create a buzz and speak effectively, and build strong relationships within professional and personal environments. By gaining experience and applying it the ability to unleash the full potential of your abilities and eliminate any communication that is not based on non-verbal authority.

IV. Perusing Others' Non-verbal communication

A. Conceiving and deciphering the appearances

1. The difference between genuine and fake smiles

Oks may provide valuable insights to an individual's thoughts and hopes. In this section we'll dive into the intricate world of smiles, and discover what distinguishes certifiable grinning grins and fake grins. There are simple indicators that distinguish a genuine smile, commonly referred to as the Duchenne smile, as distinct from an unconstrained or devious smile. If you are aware of the muscles that develop between the mouth and eyes You will be able to observe the seriousness of a smile and determine the person's their home condition in a precise manner.

In other words, a genuine smile is one that has the appearance of raising cheeks as well as the appearance of "crow's feet" wrinkles around the eyes. These expressions show the genuine joy or pleasure. On the other hand, a fake smile may not be able to show the presence of facial muscles, and appear less pronounced.

2. The facial expressions of a person's face can be used to signal if they are

Eyes convey an array of deep messages. In this section we'll look at various looks and how they relate to emotional states. It will help you figure out what you can perceive in common phrases such as joy, trouble anger, shock and the feeling of nausea. You will be able to examine specific movements and instances that are associated to every possible inclination. This will allow users to comprehend and address the underlying condition of other people in a precise manner.

A forehead that's wrinkled or fixed could indicate anger or displeasure or anger, whereas causing a ruckus and eyes that are enlarged could indicate surprise. When you are aware of these facial signals in conjunction with other non-verbal signals and signals, you'll gain better understanding of the people who have close-to-home interactions and will be better equipped to engage them with empathy and sensitivity.

www.ingramcontent.com/pod-product-compliance
Lightning Source LLC
Chambersburg PA
CBHW070554010526
44118CB00012B/1316